Phx
Local

Heroes of Fighter Command

SURREY

Rupert Matthews

COUNTRYSIDE BOOKS
NEWBURY BERKSHIRE

COUNTRYSIDE BOOKS
3 Catherine Road
Newbury, Berkshire

To view our complete range of books,
please visit us at
www.countrysidebooks.co.uk

ISBN 978 1 84674 102 9

Designed by Peter Davies, Nautilus Design

Produced through MRM Associates Ltd., Reading
Typeset by CJWT Solutions, St Helens
Printed by Information Press, Oxford

*All material for the manufacture of this book
was sourced from sustainable forests*

CONTENTS

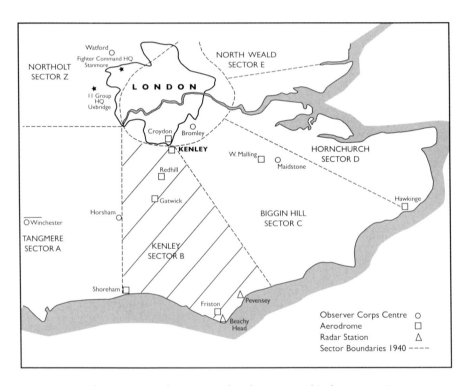

RAF Fighter Command Sectors and Fighter Control Information Centres.

Preface

I was born in Surrey, not all that far from the great fighter station of RAF Kenley – though I was not aware of it at the time. Such appreciation came only later.

As I grew up, I became aware, in my boyish way, that my father was something of a war hero. Oh, he had won no medals for gallantry or anything, but he had served in the RAF during the dark days of 1940 that I learned were known as the Battle of Britain. My father had been in RAF Bomber Command; his squadron was tasked with flying at low levels to bomb the German invasion fleet that was building up in the Channel ports. But he knew some of the men who wore the top button of their tunic jacket undone – an affectation of RAF Fighter Command.

Like most men who had served in the war, my father did not speak much about his time on the front line. I think he found it too upsetting to be reminded of all his friends who had taken off, but not come back. I picked up a few snippets of information now and then. The time the Luftwaffe had attacked his airfield and he had picked up a small injury. The time he dragged a wounded airman from a shattered aircraft that had limped home, only to find that the man died minutes later in the ambulance. The time he stood for over an hour one evening watching the darkening southern sky for a missing aircraft, and then was told it had landed – badly shot up – at a different airfield.

My father had won no medals, had been written about in no newspapers, and to many I suppose he would not qualify as a hero. But he was there when it counted. He stood up when the bullets were flying. That makes him a hero to me.

This book can mention by name only a few of the men and women who served with the RAF in Surrey during the Second World War. I have picked out a small number of exploits and events that stand out from the mass of information that has been preserved from those dark and anxious years. Some events display courage of an outstanding kind, others show how fickle can be the chances of luck in air combat, and not a few highlight the danger of it all. But it is worth remembering that anyone serving on a base of RAF Fighter Command in Surrey was heroic in a way. Whether they flew aircraft, made repairs or simply filled in the necessary paperwork they were all risking their lives. Nobody knew when German bombs were going to fall down.

I would like to thank the various RAF personnel, both serving and retired, who have helped with this book. It is probably unfair to single out anyone for special mention, but I feel that I must thank my old school friend, Squadron Leader Andrew Smith, whose enthusiasm helped to open many doors.

For my father, and all those other unsung heroes of the dark days of war, I am proud to write this book.

Introduction

RAF Fighter Command was founded on 14 July 1936, and right from the start it was obvious that Surrey was going to be one of the key counties for the new organisation. Not that either Fighter Command or Surrey were really ready for the roles allotted to them.

The Royal Air Force was, in 1936, dominated by the thinking that had come to the fore in the 1920s. Drawing on the experiences of the First World War, the staff of the RAF had come to the conclusion that the future of warfare lay with the bomber aircraft. The destructive power of large bombs dropped from specially designed aircraft was awesome. Entire factories could be destroyed by aircraft flying from bases hundreds of miles away. Battlefield targets – artillery positions, infantry trenches and the like – could similarly be obliterated with ease.

Defences against the bombers were not highly rated. Anti-aircraft fire was not effective and fighters – armed as they were with twin machine guns and able to fly only slightly faster than the bombers – were not thought capable of bringing down many intruders. The saying that 'the bomber will always get through' became almost a cliché.

Engaged as Great Britain was in a series of small-scale campaigns against colonial enemies, the RAF was allotted a secondary role to the Army and Navy. And within the RAF, the fighters were second in priority to the bombers. It is no surprise, therefore, that in the summer of 1936 the RAF could field only fifteen squadrons of fighters, nor that they were all biplane aircraft with open cockpits and modestly advanced from those that flew in the First World War.

Nevertheless, there was a growing realisation that the advent of fascist regimes in Italy, Spain and Germany, together with the growing might of Communist Russia under Stalin, might well lead to a new European war. It was not clear in 1936 what form that war might take, though it was becoming increasingly likely that Hitler's Germany was going to seek some alleviation of the terms imposed by the Treaty of Versailles that ended the First World War.

If a European war did come, then bombers could be expected to bomb British factories, British towns and British cities. It was to counter this perceived threat that Fighter Command was formed. Of the eight airfields initially allocated to the organisation, one – Kenley – was in Surrey. A second Surrey airfield – Croydon – was in civilian use but was

*A barrage balloon is prepared for launching. These balloons were tethered to the
ground over potential targets and trailed metal cables designed to catch
and bring down any aircraft that flew beneath them. The static air defences
such as these came under the control of Fighter Command.*

earmarked for immediate mobilisation as a fighter base should war be declared.

The importance of Surrey to any system of air defence of Great Britain is clear from a glance at a map. The county hugs around London to the south and south-west. Since the capital city was likely to be the prime target for enemy bombers and given the short range of defensive fighter aircraft, Surrey was clearly going to be an important base for fighters.

RAF Fighter Command was fortunate in that its first commander was an air officer of outstanding organisational abilities with a good grasp of the needs of a fighter force. Air Chief Marshal Sir Hugh Dowding was appointed in 1937, with instructions to get the new force up and running within a year. By 1939 it was clear that war with Germany was rapidly approaching. Since Dowding, who had been due to retire in 1939, was only 57, his period of command was extended by another year to July 1940, and then again to October 1940. As a result Fighter Command enjoyed a remarkable consistency of command that was not generally the case in the RAF.

As soon as he took command of Britain's aerial defences, Dowding realised that his 15 fighter squadrons, backed up by three Auxiliary Air Force units, were not going to be sufficient to protect London from the attentions of Germany's Luftwaffe. He began a massive reorganisation that was to determine the course of the air war over Surrey when the time came.

Among the measures that Dowding initiated or accelerated were the development of radar to locate and track incoming formations of enemy aircraft, the development and organisation of anti-aircraft batteries and barrage balloons, the subdivision of Fighter Command into Groups and Sectors; but above all he hurried up the development of new aircraft that were fast enough and carried enough weaponry to stand a chance of holding their own against the sophisticated German aircraft they were expected to face.

By the time war came to Surrey, the county was home to a fighting force that was second to none.

*The crew of a Bofors light anti-aircraft gun swings into action
during a practice drill. These weapons were the main form
of defence at RAF fighter bases at this time.*

Chapter 1

False Alarm

O n the day war broke out, the RAF in Surrey suffered the ignominy of having its premier airfield and command centre, RAF Kenley, entirely out of action. The fact was that the airfield was out of date, had runways too short for modern fighters and was simply not up to the task. As head of Fighter Command, Hugh Dowding had decreed that Kenley had to be closed down and fully modernised.

The work was still under way on 3 September 1939. Nevertheless, that day the station was called upon to launch a pair of fighters to intercept an incoming aircraft, thought to be a German bomber. The lone aircraft was being tracked on radar heading low and fast straight for Croydon airfield, but did not respond to any of the recognised radio signals and so was deemed to be hostile. Although the aircraft was flying alone, it caused deep worry to Dowding and others at RAF Fighter Control. The Luftwaffe was thought to have at least twice as many aircraft as the RAF, and most of them were thought to be bombers. In fact many of the German aircraft were transport or reserve aircraft, but this was not known at the time.

Dowding and others had repeatedly warned that, if massed formations of German bombers were sent all at once, the British defences would be swamped and unable to cope. It was anticipated that such a raid could easily result in the utter destruction of a city the size of Canterbury with

The main entrance to RAF Kenley as it is today. The two brick pillars are all that remain of the gateway that was here in 1940.

thousands of civilian deaths. It would take only a few such disasters for a negotiated peace to seem an attractive option to many in government.

Dowding was determined not to let this happen and wanted to give the Germans the impression that his defensive strength was greater than it was. Thus the appearance of what seemed to be a German scout probing into British airspace caused concern. The intruder had to be intercepted and destroyed as quickly as possible to send a clear message to Hermann Goering, head of the Luftwaffe, that British airspace would be defended ruthlessly.

In the event it was a false alarm. The intruder was a French transport that had forgotten to adopt the new wartime radio procedure.

That event apart, the men and women of RAF Fighter Command in Surrey had a fairly unspectacular start to the war. The prepared procedures were put in place and soon Surrey was ready for the fray. That this was so, was entirely due to the hard work and dedication of Dowding and his team. Since Fighter Command had been formed, it had been organised into four Groups, numbered 10, 11, 12 and 13. Of these 11 Group covered London and the immediately adjacent areas, so Surrey fell under this Group which was commanded by Air Vice Marshal Keith Park, a long-time colleague of Dowding. No 10 Group covered the West Country, 12 Group the Midlands and 13 Group the north of England and Scotland. As the war unfolded, it was 12 Group that would most often be called upon to cooperate with 11 Group, with results that would not always be happy for either force.

Within each Group, there were a number of Sectors. Each Sector consisted of a lead airfield where the organisation's offices were located and where there was a control room from which the Sector's squadrons would be organised when in combat. Within 11 Group, Kenley was the lead airfield for B Sector, which covered most of Surrey and adjacent parts of eastern Sussex.

This Sector system was designed to form part of the overall air defence of Britain. At the main RAF Fighter Command headquarters at RAF Bentley Priory in Middlesex, Dowding had strategic command over the

---

A Miles Master 2-seat trainer that entered service with the RAF in 1938. Most of the pilots who fought from Surrey had been trained in this type of aircraft. It was equipped with one machine gun for gunnery practice, but was never intended to take up a combat role.

The main house at RAF Bentley Priory.

whole system. He decided which squadrons were allocated where, how the anti-aircraft guns should be sited and used and where balloon barrages should be put. He also controlled both the network of radar stations that were aimed out to sea from the south and east coasts of England to detect incoming aircraft and also the hundreds of Observer Corps outposts which tracked enemy aircraft once they were over the coast and heading inland.

So that the position of RAF fighters could be determined, each aircraft was fitted with a device known as 'pip-squeak' because of the noise it made. This sent out, at regular intervals, a coded radio signal that was picked up by direction-finding receivers on the ground. Triangulation between these stations – done by hand in these early years – gave the aircraft's position.

Within each Group, the headquarters kept an overview of enemy aircraft in its area as well as what its own fighters and other defences were doing.

The control room of Fighter Command at RAF Bentley Priory as it was in September 1939. Bentley Priory was a former stately home that had been taken over by the RAF. The control room was established in the ballroom after Dowding took over Fighter Command in 1937. The room was chosen as the ceiling was high enough to allow the installation of a balcony for the controllers overlooking the situation map. Once war began, Dowding ordered the construction of a bomb-proof bunker outside the mansion for the control room.

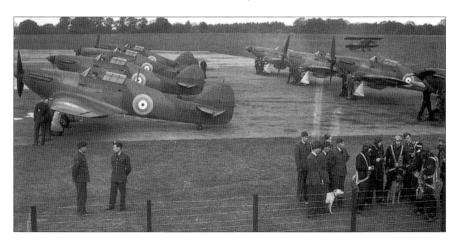

Hurricanes of No. 3 Squadron at Kenley in May 1938.

It was Group's decision when squadrons should be stood down or moved to readiness, when they should take off for patrol, when they should land to refuel and when they could go back to rest. Each Sector was responsible for collating information for the Group on the state of its squadrons and, critically, for controlling them once they were in the air.

The Sector Operations Room had within it a large map of the Sector and

WAAF Amy Mates who worked in the control room for most of 1940.

One of the few buildings at RAF Kenley to survive from the time of the Battle of Britain. This was an accommodation block for ground crew and mechanics.

adjacent areas on which were plotted the reported positions of enemy aircraft formations and the positions of RAF aircraft. The Controller sat perched so that he could look down on this map and was linked to all airborne aircraft by radio. It was his task to give fighters instructions on where to fly and at what height so that they would intercept the enemy from the most advantageous position possible. This task called for the ability to visualise the map in three dimensions, with the plotted aircraft formations at various heights. Not only that, but the position of the sun, and the depth and height of cloud formations also had to be factored in if the Controller was to do his job properly.

At Kenley all this complex and, for its time, high-tech equipment was housed in a single-storey brick structure that looked a bit like a barracks. When somebody realised that the building was entirely unprotected an earthen bank was thrown up around it to shield it from the blast of any bombs landing nearby, but it remained vulnerable to a direct hit. Only good luck would save it from obliteration in the fighting to come – that and the fact that it did not look very important from the air. In the autumn of 1940 the control room was moved off the base to the safety of an anonymous-looking civilian building over a mile away.

The job of Controller called for a knowledge and appreciation of air fighting tactics. Only then could he direct his aircraft so that they were in a position to meet the incoming German formations and also have a tactical edge that would give them the advantage in combat. Many Controllers were fighter pilots who were being rested for one reason or another.

An unnamed aircraftman photographed at Kenley in 1940. The base was home to hundreds of men who served as groundcrew, mechanics, armourers, cooks, administrative staff and payclerks.

As things stood in 1939, fighter tactics were fairly basic. It was assumed by all concerned that the RAF fighter pilots would be faced only by enemy bombers. The reasons for this were geographic. The most likely enemy was Germany and the distance from Germany was such that only bombers would be able to reach Britain.

Dowding himself did not entirely go along with this line of thinking. He had flown through the First World War and well knew that in that earlier conflict the Germans had captured large swathes of Belgium and northern France. If they repeated the feat in any future war it would give them airbases in those areas that would be within fighter range of Britain, though only just. He ordered a series of practice combats that led him to suggest to his pilots that if the German bombers had a fighter escort, then this should be attacked first by a

'Dawn Patrol', a publicity photograph put out by the RAF when war was declared. The nine fighters shown here have adopted the triple Vic formation, with each group of three aircraft formed up in a v-shape.

small decoy force that would draw the escort off so that the main force of attacking fighters would have a clear run at the bombers.

The tactics to be used when attacking bombers had been carefully formulated in the 1930s. They envisaged the enemy bombers flying in tight-knit formations so that the defensive guns of the bombers could cover each other when under attack from a deadly criss-cross of intersecting fire. To tackle these formations, the RAF fighters were to attack in successive waves of three aircraft drawn up into a Vic formation. That is, with the lead aircraft flying ahead of and slightly below the two others which flew behind the leader's wingtips. Generally, two Vics formed a flight, which was the smallest unit in which the RAF envisaged fighters operating. Two flights formed a squadron, the normal fighting unit and the basis of all administration and support services.

Attacks were thought to be best delivered from behind the enemy bomber formation. They should be delivered from above if the fighters could get the sun behind them to dazzle the enemy, or from below if not. Nobody seemed to have considered head-on attacks, probably because the closing speed of modern fighters and bombers was so far in excess of that in the First World War that such a tactic was deemed to be suicidal.

Attacks from the flank were discouraged as the difficulty of hitting a target moving sideways at around 200 mph was considered beyond the skills of most fighter pilots. Instead a new type of fighter, the turret fighter, was developed. This was a big fighter with a bomber's gun turret positioned behind the pilot. The idea was that it would fly parallel to the bomber formation while the gunner in the turret picked off enemy aircraft. The concept resulted in the Boulton Paul Defiant, but this aircraft rarely appeared over Surrey skies once the war began. The Defiant, with its lack of manoeuvrability and unusual turret-mounted guns, was too vulnerable to enemy fighters to be of much use except at night.

A formation of nine Hurricane Mk1 fighters cruises over southern England late in 1939. The tight-knit formation shown here was popular in pre-war days but the early combats with the Luftwaffe showed that a looser, more fluid formation was needed for modern air combat.

A No.17 Squadron Hurricane. The unit was in Surrey when war broke out and remained in the county until June 1940.

It was these tactics that the pilots of 1939 knew and practised. Some of those men questioned the rigidity of the tactics and suggested a more fluid form of aerial combat, but such suggestions were slapped down. Of particular concern among pilots was the insistence that the optimum range at which they should fire their guns was around 400 yards. Many believed not only that hitting a fast-moving target at such a range was unlikely, but also that the stream of bullets from their guns would be too scattered to do real damage. The official instructions were not altered, but some practised closing in much nearer to a target, sometimes to as little as 50 yards.

Among the peacetime pilots in Surrey at the time was Pilot Officer Harold Bird-Wilson, then a young pilot with 17 Squadron. This squadron was officially based at Kenley, but was under orders to move to Croydon as soon as war was declared. It had been only in June 1939 that the squadron had lost its Gloster Gauntlet II biplanes and been re-equipped with Hawker Hurricanes. It was the arrival of these modern 8-gun fighters that made the rebuilding of Kenley with all-weather concrete runways imperative. It also made the enlargement of the airfield necessary because the new monoplane fighters needed a longer runway than did the old biplanes. In the event time ran out for Kenley as the war began on 3 September.

21

Harold Bird-Wilson was based at RAF Kenley when the war broke out,
but moved to Croydon with the rest of No.17 Squadron. A peace-time civil
aviation airport, Croydon was earmarked for Fighter Command in the
event of war as early as 1937. Bird-Wilson went on to have an
adventurous career as a fighter pilot and survived the war.

Time almost ran out for Bird-Wilson in more dramatic fashion when he crashed his plane, which then erupted into a ball of flame. He suffered serious burns, especially to his uncovered face, and had to be taken to Queen Victoria Hospital in Sussex to recuperate. So bad were his burns that he lost his nose entirely. 'My fighter friends accepted me,' he later recalled, 'and so did my girlfriend. They were not put off by this embarrassing sight.' In April 1940 he had his nose reconstructed by the pioneering plastic surgeon Sir Archibald McIndoe and so qualified to join the Guinea Pig Club.

This remarkable club was at first an informal drinking club for patients undergoing reconstructive surgery for burns along with the staff who treated them. Former patients remained members, returning to the hospital for events, and by the end of the war it had 650 members including not just Britons, but also Canadians, Australians, Czechs and Poles. Unlike many military hospitals, patients were allowed to wear uniform or civilian clothes and were encouraged to venture into the town at will. East Grinstead became 'the town that did not stare'. The club still meets regularly.

Returning to action in April 1940, Bird-Wilson found himself thrown into the maelstrom of violence that accompanied the German invasions of Holland, Belgium and France. By this date his squadron was based in France, which was overrun by the rapidly advancing Nazi hordes and it was only by sheer good luck that Bird-Wilson was able to fly out, landing to refuel on the Channel Islands that were soon to fall into German hands.

During one Battle of Britain combat he was in one of 12 Hurricanes that launched a climbing attack on a formation of over 100 German bombers. His luck could not last and during one combat he was shot down into the Thames by the famous German ace Adolf Galland. This crash was horrific, the aircraft catching fire as it dived, but fortunately the new burns suffered were minor and Bird-Wilson was soon back in combat. He ended the Battle of Britain with five confirmed German aircraft to his credit.

Bird-Wilson went on to command squadrons launching sweeps over northern France and escorting bombers on daylight raids into enemy territory. He ended the war flying jet fighters and opted to remain in the RAF after the war. He then served mainly in training and tactical development posts, though he did return to active service to command the RAF units in Hong Kong for a while. He retired from the RAF in 1974 and died in 2000.

A publicity photo issued in 1939 shows a flight of Hurricane MkI fighters cruising high over the White Cliffs of Dover. By this date the RAF had 18 squadrons equipped with this fighter.

Also flying out of Kenley in the first days of war was 615 Squadron. This unit was an auxiliary squadron based in Surrey that drew most of its personnel from the county and surrounding areas. The unit went first to Croydon and then, on 15 November 1939, flew out to France to join the British forces holding the northern flank of the joint Franco-British army facing the Germans on the Western Front.

The period that followed has gone down in history as the Phoney War, due to the popular belief that not a lot happened during the winter of 1939-40. So far as major ground fighting was concerned, this impression may be valid. Once Poland surrendered, neither the British nor French saw any real need to launch a major, and no doubt costly, attack on the entrenched defences of the German army along the Franco-German border. The problem was that the only open ground suitable for a major assault was in Belgium and Holland. The governments of those countries were neutral and wanted to remain so, and so would not permit passage over their lands or through their airspace to the forces of either side.

The British and French were keen not to antagonise the neutrals, so they held back. The Germans were not so choosy. In January 1940 a transport aircraft carrying a German staff officer was forced down by heavy snow on to a Dutch airfield. With him the officer was carrying a set of plans that showed beyond doubt that the Germans were planning to invade France by way of Belgium and Holland at some time within the next few months. This prompted the Dutch and Belgians to begin planning a joint defensive plan with the British and French, though they maintained a nominal neutrality until the German invasion began. Among these plans was the move of 615 Squadron to Moorseele as soon as the invasion began so that the Hurricanes of that squadron could provide close support to bombers attacking the German assault forces.

Back in Surrey, the pace was quickening. The private flying club at Redhill was taken over by the RAF to be a training school. Among the first pupils were a group of 45 Polish pilots who had managed to escape from their country before it surrendered to the Germans. They proved to be

The pilots of a Hurricane squadron in France carry out a practice scramble for the benefit of newspaper photographers in October 1939. In fact there was very little air activity over France at this time as the Phoney War began to take a hold.

exceptional pupils, though they had trouble mastering English well enough to cope with orders and instructions given over the radio. Another non-Fighter Command airfield was at Brooklands. This was not an operational airfield, but served the nearby factory producing Wellington bombers and Hurricane fighters. The completed aircraft took off from here to be flown to the bases from which they would fly into combat.

Croydon had completed its transformation from civil airport to Fighter Command base with speed and ease. The last German airliner had left on 31 August, the airport was closed the next day and the first fighters flew in on 2 September in the form of Gladiator Is of No.615 Squadron and Hurricane Is of Nos.3 and 17 Squadrons. The airfield saw two early casualties. The first was non-fatal and occurred when a pilot returned after dark to find Croydon covered with a light ground mist. He missed the runway and came to rest on the roof of the nurses' home at nearby Purley Hospital. The second crash was more serious, costing the life of a pilot who came down for unknown reasons near Dorking.

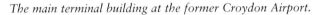

The main terminal building at the former Croydon Airport.

In December two new squadrons arrived at Croydon, Nos.92 and 145, both of which were equipped with Blenheim 1F night-fighters. At this time night-fighting was in its infancy. Not much thought had been given to the subject in pre-war years as it had been widely assumed that all bombing missions would be carried out in daylight so the bomb aimers would be able to see their targets. Consequently it was thought that fighters would fly only during the day. However, experience in the autumn of 1939 had shown that bombers were very vulnerable to fighters in daylight unless they had fighter escorts, and so bombers began to fly at night – which necessitated some sort of night-fighter response.

The Blenheim 1F was chosen as a night-fighter partly because its relatively long endurance allowed it to stooge about looking for German bombers for hours on end without needing to land to refuel. Another advantage that it had over single-engined fighters was that its three-man crew gave two additional pairs of eyes to look for the dark shape of a German bomber against a dark sky. The Blenheim was also chosen as the RAF had several hundred of these aircraft that had been bought as long-range day-fighters but had proved to be obsolete compared to the German Messerschmitt fighters they were called upon to tackle.

As yet the Blenheim was merely an experimental night-fighter. The squadrons based at Croydon spent their time training to home in accurately on fixes given by radar stations so that should German bombers come in large numbers by night the RAF would be able to intercept them with some measure of reliability. Doing this was difficult work and even with practice few crews could achieve the task with any real success. It was with relief that some pilots found themselves transferred back to day-fighter squadrons.

One such pilot was Roger Bushell, a 30-year-old South African and former world champion downhill skier. Bushell had been an auxiliary pilot, training for combat flying when not at his day job as a criminal barrister in London. When war was declared he was called up and, due to his excellent flying record and many hours of combat practice, he was made a squadron leader. He proved to be an excellent leader of men and a ferocious advocate of relentless training and preparation. Unfortunately, at 30, he was a bit old to be a fighter pilot as his reflexes had begun to slow, not by much but by enough to make a split second difference in the whirling mayhem of aerial combat. During only his second combat mission Bushell was shot down behind German lines.

For others this might have been the end of a short, but reasonably good career with the RAF. Not for Bushell. It turned out to be the start of a new and altogether more impressive phase of his life that would win him enduring fame and ultimately led to his death. Bushell became an expert escaper.

Arriving at the prisoner-of-war camp, Dulag Luft, Bushell was put in charge of questioning new arrivals. This process both supplied the inmates with the latest news from home, and served to identify any 'stool pigeons' – English-speaking Germans pretending to be prisoners. He also joined the camp's Escape Committee, rising rapidly to be its deputy chief. He dug two tunnels during the summer of 1940, but one was discovered by guards and the second was flooded out. In spring 1941 he began a third tunnel, but before it was completed he escaped from the camp by hiding until after dark in the hut which housed the commandant's goat, and then walking off. Pretending to be a Swiss tourist – he could speak reasonably good German – Bushell got as far as the Swiss border before an alert guard spotted his passport was a fake. Meanwhile his tunnel was completed and 24 men got out, most being recaptured within a few days.

Sent to a camp at Lübeck, Bushell joined the Escape Committee and began another tunnel. This was incomplete when he was told he and other inmates were being moved. On the train to the new camp, Bushell and a Czech named Zaphok cut a hole in the floor. They dropped out as the train slowed for a hill. Once out of the train the pair adopted civilian clothes and headed for Prague carrying fake identity papers. The pair were staying with friends of Zaphok when the brutal German governor of Czech lands, Reinhard Heydrich, was murdered by the Czech resistance. The Gestapo moved in to round up anyone even remotely suspicious. Bushell and Zaphok were soon singled out and arrested. When they realised that Bushell was British, the Gestapo assumed that he was a member of the British secret service sent to organise the Heydrich assassination. Bushell was subjected to a brutal interrogation by the Gestapo before the Germans realised that he was an escaped prisoner of war unconnected to the killing. The Gestapo released him, but as he left told him that if he fell into their hands again they would kill him.

Having recovered from his experiences with the Gestapo, Bushell was sent to Stalag Luft III, a POW camp in the far east of Germany. As the most famous escaper held in Germany, Bushell was put in charge of the Escape Committee. Group Captain Herbert Massey, the senior British officer at the camp heard about the Gestapo threat and refused to allow Bushell to escape, designating him 'Big X' to hide his role in escape attempts from the Germans.

Nevertheless, it was at Stalag Luft III that Bushell embarked on his greatest achievement: The Great Escape. After spending some months probing the German security for weaknesses, Bushell announced to the Escape Committee that he wanted to dig three major tunnels through which 250 men could escape in a single night, each man dressed in civilian clothes and carrying forged papers, maps of escape routes and with enough rudimentary German to pass as foreign workers from France or Italy on their way home. He concluded his presentation of the plan with these words: 'Everyone here in this room is living on borrowed time. By rights we should all be dead! The only reason that God allowed us this extra ration of life is so we can make life hell for the Hun. In North Compound we are concentrating our efforts on completing and escaping through one master tunnel. No private-enterprise tunnels allowed. Three bloody deep, bloody long tunnels will be dug – Tom, Dick, and Harry. One will succeed!' The speech was followed by a stunned silence. Nothing on this scale had ever been considered before, let alone tried. In the event, everyone agreed and the plan got under way.

The entire camp was called upon to help, though nobody outside the Escape Committee knew exactly what was going on. Some men sewed civilian clothes, others forged papers, some kept watch for German guards and a large number were tasked with getting rid of the soil dug up out of the tunnels.

For months the work went on. One tunnel was discovered and a second abandoned, but 'Harry' was completed by mid-March 1944. On the 24th the escape went ahead. Unfortunately the tunnel emerged in the wrong place and was spotted by a German sentry after only 76 men had got away. Bushell was travelling with a French officer named Lieutenant Bernard Scheidhauer, both posing as French commercial travellers heading home after a business trip to Germany. Bushell and Scheidhauer opted to travel by train but were arrested on 26 March when Bushell's ID card was seen to be out of date by a sharp-eyed guard at Saarbrücken.

Bushell was, at first, held by the local police and was put into a cell with a handful of other escapees. Once the Gestapo learned that Bushell had been caught, Obersturmbannführer Dr. Leopold Spann, the Saarbrücken Gestapo chief, was sent to take charge. On 29 March Spann and his

Gloster Gladiator

Type:	Single seat fighter
Engine:	840 hp Bristol Mercury
Wingspan:	32 ft 3 in
Length:	27 ft 5 in
Height:	10 ft 4 in
Weight:	Empty 3450 lb
	Loaded 4750 lb

Armament: 4 x 0.303 machine guns in nose and under wings
Max speed: 253 mph
Ceiling: 33,000 ft
Range: 428 miles
Production: 768

The Gladiator was the last biplane to enter service with the RAF, first reaching squadrons in February 1937. Despite its outdated appearance the Gladiator was in many ways a most advanced aircraft. It had a fully enclosed cockpit, a metal propeller and a relatively heavy armament. By the time war broke out Fighter Command had removed the Gladiator from front line service, although it was retained for local use – six of the Gladiators were stationed at Plymouth docks to protect them for instance. In 1940 three Gladiators – nicknamed Faith, Hope and Charity – guarded Malta against the massed raids of the Italian air force. By 1942 the Gladiator had left combat duties, being relegated to gathering meteorological data.

The first Gladiator entered service with No.72 Squadron and soon after with No.3 Squadron. Gladiators assigned to Nos.607 and 615 Squadrons were despatched to France in September 1939 to reinforce the four Hurricane MkI-equipped squadrons already assigned to the Air Component of the British Expeditionary Force and which had suffered heavy losses. During the Battle of Britain, No.247 Squadron based at Roborough was the sole surviving operational Gladiator unit; a last link with the eighteen other home-based squadrons that had operated the RAF's last biplane fighter during the late 1930s.

Bristol Blenheim 1F

Type: Three seat night-fighter
Engine: 2 x 840 hp Bristol Mercury
Wingspan: 56 ft 4 in
Length: 39 ft 9 in
Height: 9 ft 10 in
Weight: Empty 8840 lb
Loaded 12,500 lb
Armament: 6 x 0.303 machine guns in nose and upper turret
Max speed: 278 mph
Ceiling: 26,000 ft
Range: 1050 miles
Production: 1,427

The Bristol Blenheim in all its various models began life as a light civilian passenger aircraft called the Britain First, or more prosaically the Type 142. The RAF saw the potential of the model and ordered it first as a light bomber and then as a long-range fighter. As a fighter it was manoeuvrable and fast, by the standards of 1937 when it entered service, and had good visibility. By 1940, however, its allotted role of long-range escort to daylight bombers had proven to be abortive as it was too vulnerable to the Messerschmitt Bf109. The fighter version was therefore switched to the newly emerging night-fighter role which it fulfilled until early 1942. The photo above shows a Blenheim IV bomber. The bombers were moved to the Mediterranean and the colonies, but were gradually phased out of front-line service to be reserved for training and other duties.

The first Blenheim 1fs were delivered to No.600 Squadron at RAF Hendon in September 1938. By mid-1940, six Fighter Command units had received the type, with No.23 Squadron carrying out the first night intruder sortie on the night of 21/22 December 1939. On 18 May 1940, five Luftwaffe bombers were downed in what proved to be the Blenheim 1f's most successful single sortie. The first 'kill' by a radar-equipped Blenheim 1f came on the night of 2/3 July and involved an aircraft operated by the Fighter Interception Unit based at Ford.

assistant Emil Schultz arrived at the prison with papers authorising them to take charge of Bushell and Scheidhauer for transport to Mannheim where they would he handed over to the prisoner-of-war authorities. The pair were bundled into a limousine driven by Walter Breithaupt and set off on the Mannheim road. After about 25 miles they reached a wooded area where Spann told Breithaupt to stop so that everyone could stretch their legs and relieve themselves. While Breithaupt smoked by the car Bushell and Scheidhauer stepped a few yards to a bush. Spann and Schultz followed as if they too would relieve themselves. Instead they pulled guns and shot the two prisoners in the back of the head. The bodies were bundled back into the car and the badly rattled driver ordered to head for Neue Bremm where the bodies were dumped at a concentration camp for disposal.

Of the 76 men who escaped, 50 were shot dead on Hitler's personal instructions. Many more of those who escaped or who had built the tunnel would have been shot had not Goering stepped in to stop the killings.

In 1945, after Germany surrendered, the RAF sent a team to investigate the deaths of the 50 men. Up until then the Gestapo had said only that the men had 'been shot while attempting to escape'. Breithaupt came forward to give a full statement of what had happened to Bushell, allowing the investigators to pinpoint Spann as the man who had organised the killings. He had been killed during an air raid early in 1945, but several of his gunmen were subsequently arrested, tried and hanged.

All such brutality lay far in the future as the bright yellow daffodils of spring poked their heads above the ground in early 1940. What was clear was that with the good weather the war would very soon be hotting up. And Dowding was a worried man – with good reason.

Chapter 2

Action Stations!

By April 1940 it was clear that a major German assault on France, probably by way of Belgium and Holland, was imminent. The joint British-French military staffs believed that they had the situation well in hand and that they were up to the threat. Even Winston Churchill, who had been warning for years about the massive military build up of Nazi Germany, was quietly confident. A few others were not so certain. One of them was Hugh Dowding, head of RAF Fighter Command.

The conventional view was that the Germans would attack along a fairly broad frontage, swinging through central Belgium and southern Holland. This would allow them to deploy their panzers and artillery to good effect, avoiding the heavily defended Franco-German border and – if the assault went far enough – outflanking the main British and French armies grouped around Sedan and Metz.

The Allies planned to counter this by moving their main armies further north, then marching directly into Belgium to meet the German advance head on somewhere in the region of Namur or Antwerp. In this way the German forces, moving forward on a broad front, would be met by forces just as strong as their own taking up a defensive stance on ground of the Allies' choosing. The Germans would be held on this forward line, or if not, on a reserve line around Lille. Once the main German thrust had been stopped, a counterattack would be delivered to drive them back. If the counterattack did not work, it would not matter too much. In the First World War, Germany had had Turkey and the Austro-Hungarian Empire as allies but had still lost. In 1940, Germany was alone and could not hope – the Allies thought – to maintain the stress and expense of total war for more than six months or a year.

The problem with this plan, as Dowding saw it, was that it was an 'all or nothing' scheme. So long as the first German assault was halted at Namur, Antwerp or at Lille all would be well. But there was no back-up plan if the Germans were not halted in those positions during the first ten days of their attack. Given that Dowding's task was to defend Britain from air attack he had a rather different perspective on the coming campaign than did the generals, and most politicians, who were concentrating on the coming ground battles.

Dowding had estimated before the war that he would need at least 53 squadrons of modern fighters to defend Britain against the Luftwaffe. When war broke out he had only 35 ready for combat. Four of those squadrons were sent to France to support British ground troops in September 1939. A few weeks later he was ordered to send two more, but managed to palm off the French with two squadrons of biplane Gladiators. In the spring of 1940 he was ordered to send two more squadrons and have two others ready to go if needed.

One of the key problems with sending fighter squadrons to France was wastage. There was very little actual fighting over the winter, but numerous aircraft had to be sent back for maintenance as they were wearing out. The French had kept all the good airfields for their own air force and given the RAF squadrons commandeered private clubs where facilities ran to little more than a flattish grass runway and a hangar or two. The valuable and relatively fragile fighter aircraft suffered from bouncing over bumpy ground, being stored in canvas hangars and being maintained in muddy fields. The men, forced to sleep under canvas in below-freezing temperatures, fared little better. Many of Dowding's precious replacement fighters, pilots and engineers had to be sent out to France to replace those unable to continue.

Moreover, Dowding was becoming seriously worried about the ability of his Fighter Command to defend the air space over Britain – which was its primary duty after all. When he raised his concerns and doubts he was brushed aside and told not to worry. The French had a large and modern air force, he was told, so the German Luftwaffe would have its hands full

A Gloster Gladiator of 615 Squadron, 1940.

there and would be unable to turn their main strength against Britain. Dowding was unconvinced, but as a good serviceman he followed his orders to keep the British forces in France supplied with adequate fighter cover.

In Surrey, meanwhile, the situation had been improving. Kenley had partly reopened in January 1940 when the concrete runways were completed, though the taxiways and enlarged buildings were not ready until some weeks later. By the end of April Kenley was fully open for business. A few weeks earlier, Croydon had lost its Blenheim night-fighters to gain a squadron of Spitfires and another of Hurricanes. Gatwick was handed over to Bomber Command.

In early May German aircraft began to probe the skies over France in much larger numbers than ever before. Combats escalated, as did losses. The senior air officers in France sent back messages to Dowding advising him that all fighter aircraft should have bullet-proof armour fitted to the back of the pilot's seat as the Germans so often launched attacks from

A pilot of No.1 Squadron clambers into a Hurricane parked in a blast shelter. The squadron was in Surrey for most of 1941.

above and behind. They were in the process of drawing up a report on other lessons learnt, but it was all too late.

On 10 May, just before dawn, the Luftwaffe swarmed over the border and flew on deep into France. The pilots came armed not only with bombs and bullets, but also with detailed and accurate maps of the airfields of the French air force. By mid-morning the French air force had ceased to exist as a coherent fighting force. The Luftwaffe ruled the skies.

The RAF squadrons in France at first escaped lightly. Based as they were on a hotch-potch of small, private airfields they had not attracted the attention of the Luftwaffe. That was soon to change as the British aircraft climbed up to face the incoming German bombers. Deprived of the supposedly large and effective French air force, the British aircraft were hopelessly outnumbered. Very many bombers and fighters were shot down.

One of the squadrons earmarked to go out to France when the land fighting began was No.3 Squadron, based at Kenley. One of the star pilots of the squadron was Pilot Officer Frank Carey, who had joined the squadron as a Sergeant Pilot in 1939 and been commissioned as a result of his courage and leadership skills. Carey first went into action on

30 January. The squadron had been sent to intercept German bombers attacking a coastal convoy of merchant ships. Arriving over the battle, Carey followed his section leader in a screaming attack. Closing to short range, Carey held his fire until the enemy bomber filled his sights, then let rip with a devastating cone of machine-gun fire that sent the German diving down into the sea alongside the ship it had been trying to sink.

Four days later Carey was again sent up to protect a convoy, this time flying as section leader. As they approached, the Hurricanes were spotted by the German bombers which began to turn away, heading for a bank of low cloud that would hide them from the British fighter pilots. Carey was too quick for them. On his own initiative he lowered the nose of his fighter to gain speed and swooped past the bombers to get between them and the cloud cover. Although he did not shoot down an enemy aircraft in this combat, his quick action made the Germans dive towards a different area of cloud cover, giving his comrades time to attack and shoot two down.

A No.402 Squadron Hurricane cruises over southern England. The squadron was in Surrey several times during the war, most notably for much of 1942, and flew both Hurricanes and Spitfires.

As he took off for France, the newly-promoted Pilot Officer Carey led his section. In the hectic days of fighting that followed Carey shot down five more German aircraft. 'This officer, by his dash and courage, set the highest example of gallantry to the squadron,' wrote his commander on 31 May when recommending him for a DFC to add to the DFM he had already won.

Carey was to be one of those men who attract action. When he came back from France, he was posted to Scotland, then to Yorkshire to spend a few months in a quiet sector to recuperate from the stress of the fighting in France. In both places the Germans launched major raids from Norway soon after his arrival. Carey shot down four more enemy aircraft and was awarded a bar to his DFC. Promoted to Wing Commander, Carey was in 1941 sent out to Burma just in time to be hit by the Japanese invasion of that country. In March 1942 he was awarded a second bar to his DFC for his courageous fighting and magnificent leadership qualities in Burma – where he shot down five Japanese bombers.

Flying out to France alongside Carey in May 1940 was another young pilot of No.3 Squadron, Flight Lieutenant Walter Churchill. By the time he came back a few short weeks later he had shot down three German aircraft and been awarded the DFC and the Distinguished Service Order (DSO).

It wasn't only in the air that things were going badly for the Allies. The German ground advance was progressing more quickly than expected. No.615 (Surrey) Squadron was supposed to move forward to the Belgian airfield at Evere when the Germans attacked in order to support British army units hurrying towards Namur. As the first aircraft of No.615 came down to land at Evere they found themselves faced by rifle fire from German troops already occupying the airfield. Opening throttles the aircraft roared back into the sky to return to France.

By 12 May the German armies were streaming into Belgium and Holland on a broad front, just as predicted. The British and French armies marched forward to meet them, just as predicted. What had not been predicted was that the French air force would be a mass of smoking wreckage by this date. The French asked the British to send over more aircraft to face the Luftwaffe. Dowding refused. Instead he put refuelling depots on the airfields the RAF were using, sending squadrons over from England for the day but bringing them back in the evening.

The toll that these day missions could take was shown on 18 May when 12 Hurricanes from RAF Kenley flew out to France. They landed at the

A pair of No.610 Squadron Spitfires on patrol.

small airfield of Vitry en Artois to refuel. Minutes later the Luftwaffe launched a devastating raid that destroyed seven of the 12 aircraft. None of the pilots were killed and all got home by sea, but the loss of the aircraft was a serious blow.

Flying out of Kenley was Flying Officer William Gore. Leading a dawn mission over the Channel to patrol the coast he came across three Heinkel 111 bombers flying in formation. Gore led his patrol into the attack and all three bombers were shot down. Unfortunately for Gore, just as he turned for home his engine suddenly erupted into flames and seized. Taking to his parachute he floated down to land behind Allied lines and returned to England by ship.

Meanwhile something else that had not been predicted by anybody on the Allied side was happening to the south of the main action at Sedan. A huge force of German panzers and motorised infantry had crossed the river Meuse on 12 May. The French troops guarding the river crossing had been heavily outnumbered and fled after a short battle. The panzers stormed forward, while the Luftwaffe swarmed overhead. Not only did the German aircraft attack any Allied troops they saw but they also prevented Allied aircraft from flying over the area to see what was happening. Reports came in putting the German panzers as far west as Rethel and Signy, but everything was confusion.

By the evening of 14 May one thing was terribly clear. A massive force of panzers had broken through the French lines at Sedan and was heading west at great speed. Further north the British commander in France, Lord Gort, pulled his men back from the planned forward position by a few miles.

In fact there were some 50 divisions of German armoured troops thundering through the Sedan gap. The Germans were not advancing on the anticipated broad front at all. Instead they were pushing forward on a very narrow front to punch through the Allied lines with the intention of penetrating right into the most vulnerable rear areas before fanning out to disrupt Allied supply lines, smash communications and crush the Allies piecemeal. The panzers were all linked to each other by radio, as were the Luftwaffe bombers and fighters. A sophisticated system of coordination allowed the ground troops to call up air support whenever they ran into resistance. The combination of narrow advances in strength, fast moving armoured troops and close air support was an entirely new way of waging war. It would go down in history as 'blitzkrieg'.

In May 1940, blitzkrieg was new and unexpected. Very few people outside a relatively small group of German officers really understood it. One man who did was the French Prime Minister Paul Reynaud. In the pre-war years he had taken an interest in tanks and by midnight on 14 May he had enough information on his desk to realise what the Germans were up to, and to see that

Lord Gort was the commander of the British forces in France when the German blitzkrieg struck in 1940. It was he who gave the order to evacuate to Dunkirk and who called upon the RAF to provide air cover for the evacuation. He was later governor of first Gibraltar and then Malta. Promoted to the rank of Field Marshal, he died in 1946.

it was succeeding. At dawn on 15 May Reynaud phoned Winston Churchill, by now Prime Minister of Britain, and brushing aside any pleasantries, Reynaud delivered his stark message to Churchill – 'We have lost the war'.

Churchill refused to believe Reynaud. He had quite different reports from Lord Gort, whose British troops were holding their own in the north, with relative ease. He had also had requests from the French military commanders asking for more British aircraft to be sent to France. Churchill called a cabinet meeting for 15 May and asked Dowding to attend to take part in the discussions.

Dowding arrived early and sat waiting until the cabinet discussions reached air matters. He was then called in and sat a few seats from Churchill. The discussion began as Churchill outlined the confused and often contradictory reports about the military situation that were coming out of France. He then explained that the French military were asking for more RAF fighters to be sent to France to counter the Luftwaffe. Then he turned to Dowding and asked his opinion.

This was the moment that Dowding had been waiting for. He announced that in the previous three days around 200 Hurricanes had been lost fighting over France. He pointed out that if France surrendered and Britain fought on then the entire Luftwaffe would be unleashed on Britain. He explained that he already had far fewer fighters than he needed. He then displayed a graph that plotted recent losses in France against replacements and continued the line forward for two weeks. 'If the present losses continue for another fortnight,' he said, 'we will not have a single Hurricane left in France *or in this country*.' The cabinet agreed that no more fighters were to go to France. Not content with that, Dowding typed up a letter when he returned to Bentley Priory that summarised his case and confirmed the decision. Then he began to concentrate on getting his surviving men and machines home.

Among the squadrons to be brought back at speed was No.615, which returned to Kenley. By the time the unit returned its commander, Squadron Leader John Kayle, had shot down four German aircraft over France. He was awarded the Distinguished Flying Cross. King George VI himself came down to Kenley for the day to make the presentation. Also decorated that day was Flight Lieutenant James Sanders of the same squadron. He had accounted for three German aircraft over France.

Another of the squadrons to come to Surrey after fighting over France

Air Chief Marshal Sir Hugh Dowding commanded RAF Fighter Command throughout the Battle of Britain. He had served in the Royal Flying Corps from 1914-18 and in the RAF thereafter. He was a highly experienced combat pilot with an instinctive feel for the needs of his men.

was No.501 which came to Croydon to recover from its losses. One of the 'aces' of the unit was Sergeant James Lacey. At this time an ace was a pilot with five confirmed victims to his credit. It was normal for a fighter pilot who reached this score to be given a medal of some kind. Lacey had been recommended for a Distinguished Flying Medal (DFM) when he downed his fifth victim over France. In the rush to get away, however, the paperwork seems to have been lost. It was not until some weeks later that his commanding officer began to wonder where the medal had got to and chased it up. Lacey eventually got his 'gong' in August 1940, by which time he had shot down a sixth German aircraft.

Also landing at Croydon was No.111 Squadron – badly battered by the French campaign. Among the veterans in that unit was Flying Officer Henry Ferriss. On 15 May he had been sent up to tackle a formation of German bombers, but had been attacked by several Messerschmitt Bf110 twin-engine fighters. Using what his squadron commander called 'outstanding ability', Ferriss turned inside the Germans and shot two of them down. The next day he was sent up and shot down two more German fighters. In the following five days he downed three additional German aircraft, and so came home to England with seven kills to his credit.

Dowding was not the only one to have become convinced that France was finished. Lord Gort was even then planning how to evacuate his army from France. By 19 May he had decided to use the port of Dunkirk, but did not yet order the evacuation to begin as the French Commander-in-Chief, Marshal Weygand, promised him that a massive French counter-attack was about to take place. By 23 May the French attack had not begun, so Gort ordered his army to fall back 25 miles to a new defensive position. Two days later there was still no sign of the promised French attack. Gort ordered the Dunkirk evacuation to begin. The Royal Navy had been drawing up plans to get the soldiers out of Europe and put to sea as soon as they received the message from Gort. Neither Churchill nor the Cabinet had yet authorised the move, but the military men knew speed was of the essence.

Air cover was vital too. Dowding was asked to send fighters over to Dunkirk to protect the army and navy from the Luftwaffe. This time, with British lives at stake in the most savage of circumstances, Dowding did not hesitate. Even though he knew he was denuding his defences, Dowding sent his aircraft over the Channel. They fought hard battles against the

Luftwaffe over Dunkirk, over the sea and for some miles inland. The fighter pilots found that, operating so far from their bases, they had only enough fuel for a few minutes combat over Dunkirk before they had to head home again. Down on the ground the soldiers being bombed and strafed by German aircraft complained that the RAF was not doing their bit. The criticism was unfair, but firmly believed.

Fighter aircraft from Surrey were putting in extra long missions, landing first at bases in Kent to refuel before heading east to Dunkirk. Among those flying these arduous missions was Sergeant Geoffrey Allard. He had seen no fighting before his squadron went out to France, but he was then pitched into the whirlwind of combat. He first went into action on 10 May and by 13 May had four confirmed kills. By 20 May he had downed a

---

The letter sent by Dowding to the government to confirm the results of the fateful Cabinet meeting at which he had persuaded Churchill not to send any more fighters to France as the German panzer breakthrough took place. This framed copy of the letter hung on the wall of his office in Bentley Priory in 2007.

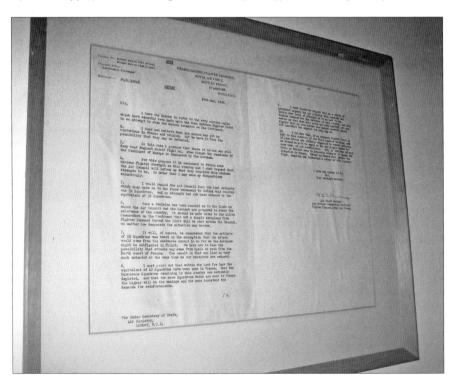

total of 10 confirmed German aircraft and had claimed five more, though these remained unconfirmed due to the confused nature of the campaign. He found the fighting over Dunkirk more trying, operating as he was at extreme range, but he managed to shoot down another German all the same.

By midnight on 2 June it was all over. In all 224,000 British troops had been evacuated. A small rearguard had been left behind to hold off German attacks, then surrender. A few British units and RAF squadrons had been elsewhere in France when the German assault began. At first they were moved up to join the new French defensive line south of the river Somme, but when that collapsed in early June they hurried to escape by way of western French ports.

On 14 June the Germans marched into Paris unopposed. The French government had abandoned the capital and headed south. The French army had abandoned the city for fear that street fighting might mar the beauty of the French capital. Two days later the Germans were on the banks of the Rhône and the Loire. That day Churchill asked the French to continue the war from the secure bases of their overseas colonies. The French government refused and instead asked the Germans for an armistice pending a full surrender.

It was now only a matter of time before the full might of the Luftwaffe would be thrown at Britain – and Surrey was going to be right in the front line.

Hawker Hurricane

Type: Single-seat fighter
Engines: 1030 hp Rolls Royce Merlin
Wingspan: 40 ft
Length: 31 ft 5 in
Height: 13 ft
Weight: Empty 4982 lb
Loaded 6532 lb
Armament: 8 x 0.303 machine guns in wings
Max speed: 324 mph
Ceiling: 34,200ft
Range: 600 miles
Production: 14,449

The first of the low-wing monoplane fighters to enter service with the RAF, the Hurricane was a vast improvement on any other aircraft then in British service. When war came it quickly proved itself to be a reliable fighter in combat conditions. It was beloved by its pilots as a 'steady gun platform' and was frequently employed to tackle German bombers while the more agile Spitfires dealt with the fighters. The figures given above relate to the Hurricane MkI, the version that fought through the Battle of Britain. By 1941 the MkII was entering service with an uprated 1460 hp Merlin engine and consequent improvements in performance. This MkII could carry a range of armament, including 12 machine guns or four 20 mm cannon. The MkIIC could carry either 1,000 lb of bombs or racks of rockets and was known informally as the 'Hurribomber'. The Hurricane was still in service when the war ended in 1945.

Service use of the Hurricane MkI, 3,834 of which were built, began with No.111 Squadron in December 1937. By the outbreak of war, 497 had been delivered and equipped a total of eighteen squadrons in Fighter Command. On 10 July 1940, Hurricanes equipped 29 squadrons in 10–13 Groups; average strength in Hurricanes during the Battle of Britain was 1,326, compared with 957 Spitfire MkIs.

Messerschmitt Bf109

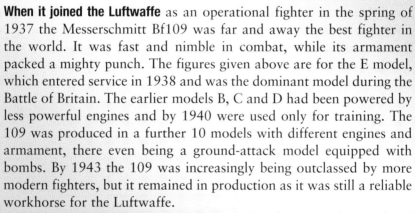

Type: Single-seat fighter
Engines: 1175 hp Daimler Benz DB601Aa
Wingspan: 32 ft 4 in
Length: 28 ft
Height: 8 ft 2 in
Weight: Empty 4189 lb
Loaded 5875 lb
Armament: 2 x 20 mm cannon plus 2 x 7.9 mm machine guns
Max speed: 348 mph
Ceiling: 34,450 ft
Range: 410 miles
Production: 35,000

When it joined the Luftwaffe as an operational fighter in the spring of 1937 the Messerschmitt Bf109 was far and away the best fighter in the world. It was fast and nimble in combat, while its armament packed a mighty punch. The figures given above are for the E model, which entered service in 1938 and was the dominant model during the Battle of Britain. The earlier models B, C and D had been powered by less powerful engines and by 1940 were used only for training. The 109 was produced in a further 10 models with different engines and armament, there even being a ground-attack model equipped with bombs. By 1943 the 109 was increasingly being outclassed by more modern fighters, but it remained in production as it was still a reliable workhorse for the Luftwaffe.

As the Luftwaffe's principal fighter aircraft during the Battle of Britain, 934 Bf109Es (805 of which were serviceable) equipped no less than 23 Gruppen in eight Jagdgeschwaders by mid-August 1940, operating from eighteen bases in northern France, Belgium and the Netherlands. In addition, one Staffel of Erprobugsgruppe 210 used Bf109Es in the fighter-bomber role. A total of 610 'Emils' fell to British guns between July and October 1940, but this potent fighter also accounted for the vast majority of the 1,172 aircraft lost by RAF Fighter Command during the same period.

Chapter 3

The Gathering Storm

The fall of France had a catastrophic effect as far as RAF Fighter Command in Surrey was concerned. Britain was now alone facing Germany. The French army had surrendered, so had the French fleet and what little was left of the French air force was in German hands. When the war had begun in the autumn of 1939, Britain had had Poland and France as allies. Between the three of them they outnumbered Germany in everything that appeared to count: men, weapons, money and natural resources. But Germany had the key advantages of new tactics, new weapons and the skills to use them. Now Britain was outnumbered – and for RAF Fighter Command it was even worse.

The whole system of air defence of Britain had been based on the assumption that the most likely enemy was Germany and that Germany was so far away that bombers would be arriving without fighter escort. But under the terms of the surrender that the French had just signed, all French air force bases were handed over to the Luftwaffe. Many of those bases were in northern France, ideally placed to send air raids over the Channel to Britain. Crucially that put most of southern England within fighter range of the new Luftwaffe bases. The bombers would be coming with fighter escorts.

But, at first, the German bombers did not come. Dowding breathed a sigh of relief and set about reforming his defences for the battle that he

A pair of No.611 Squadron Spitfires patrolling over southern England.

knew was to follow. A key difference was that while bomber attacks had been expected to come from the east, from Germany over the North Sea, they could now be expected to come from France to the south.

Surrey had been earmarked to provide support to the front line squadrons in Kent. Now it was going to lie right under the bomber flight path to London and could be expected to be a major battleground in its own right. Fortunately the chain of radar stations had already been extended along the south coast, providing the RAF with valuable warning of incoming raids, but the system had not yet been perfected or tested.

Dowding knew that he was going to lose a lot of pilots and aircraft in the combats to come. An appeal was sent out to the aircraft factories producing Spitfires and Hurricanes, and output was stepped up. A network of civilian workshops was established to repair badly damaged aircraft. This took pressure off the RAF maintenance crews at the airbases, allowing them to concentrate on quick patch and mend repairs of lightly damaged aircraft. In this way there was not only an increased supply of new aircraft, but damaged fighters could return to the fray more speedily.

The Hawker Hurricane MkI, seen here in pre-war markings, was the first monoplane fighter to enter service with RAF Fighter Command. The first production aircraft were delivered to the RAF in December 1937.

Pilot numbers proved to be more of a problem. It took many months to train a fighter pilot in the skills needed to be effective in the deadly art of air-to-air combats. The pilots coming out of the training programme in the summer of 1940 had started in the previous winter. The only way to speed up the supply was to shorten the training programme, which would mean putting men into battle when they were not yet fully trained. At first, Dowding turned this method down as it would have been almost suicidally dangerous for the young pilots concerned. Later pressure would change his mind.

By the middle of July 1940, Dowding should have had 19 squadrons of Spitfires, 25 of Hurricanes and 8 of other types. There were in all some 1,132 Spitfires and Hurricanes on the Fighter Command books; but of those, 159 had only just arrived from factories and had not yet been worked up to operational status and another 200 or so were being repaired or were out of action for routine maintenance. Some pilots were sick, injured or away on leave (which would soon be cancelled). As a result Dowding actually had just 660 fighters ready for action.

*The Kenley section of the squadron situation board in the control room of 11 Group
bunker at RAF Uxbridge. The position of the coloured lights indicated the
condition of the squadron: Released; Available 30 minutes; Available; Ordered to
Readiness; At Readiness; At Standby; Ordered on Patrol; Left Ground; In Position;
Detailed to Raid; Enemy Sighted; Ordered to Land; Landed and Refuelling.*

And still the only German aircraft heading for Britain were lone bombers and long-range fighters. They seemed to be, and were, probing the defences to see how quickly the RAF reacted to an intrusion, or carrying out reconnaissance flights over coastal areas.

The reason for the lull in the fighting was that Hitler had expected Britain to come to terms once her allies had been crushed. The conquest of Britain, or France for that matter, had no real place in his plans for German expansion. All Hitler asked of the western powers was that they stood aside while he reconfigured the map of eastern Europe, massively increased German wealth and power and subjected the conquered peoples of the east to near slave conditions. Britain, of course, was not prepared to do that. Churchill had clearly foreseen German expansion under Hitler and was convinced that neither Hitler nor Germany would be content to have hegemony over eastern Europe. Britain, France and others would be next to feel the none-too-subtle pressure of the Nazi jackboot. Alone and unaided, Britain would fight on.

It took a few days for Hitler to realise that Britain would not give in, and to realise that his military had no clear plan on how to defeat Britain. The German navy wanted to launch a naval war in the Atlantic, sinking the ships bringing supplies to Britain and so starving her into surrender. They estimated that this would take a year or so, would require considerable air support and would necessitate the building of hundreds of U-boats.

The army on the other hand wanted to invade Britain, subjecting the island nation to the same blitzkrieg tactics that had crushed Poland and France. They pointed out that most of the British army's tanks and artillery had been left behind at Dunkirk. Britain was virtually defenceless. They estimated that Britain could be defeated within a month of the panzers getting ashore.

Hitler, keen to return to his plans for eastern Europe, backed the army. Britain would be invaded in September 1940. That decision led to immediate dispute between the army and navy about how best to go about the invasion. The German army wanted to land on a wide front to confuse the defenders, but to put the main force into two key thrusts striking deep inland. The German navy, worried about the Royal Navy's larger fleet, refused saying that they could guarantee to guard only a small area of the English Channel so that the attack would need to be restricted to only the two main forces.

On one thing both army and navy were agreed. No invasion could take place unless the RAF was first knocked out. The threat from RAF bombers to both ships and panzers was too great to be ignored. The Luftwaffe had performed a similar duty in Poland and in France, destroying their air forces largely on the ground on the first day of the invasion and finishing them off in the days that followed, the Luftwaffe having by then established an early and clear aerial superiority.

Goering was confident that he could do the same to the RAF. The British Spitfire and Hurricane fighters were good, but not noticeably more so than the Potez or Bloch aircraft that had equipped the French air force. As in Poland and France, the Luftwaffe had good maps of where RAF bases were located in Britain and which aircraft were based where. Pre-war Luftwaffe men had been frequent passengers on German civilian flights to and from Britain, not a few of which had strayed off their flight path to pass close to RAF bases. Finally Goering had fairly accurate estimates of RAF strength that showed him that the Luftwaffe had a clear advantage in all types of aircraft.

The first Luftwaffe sorties were designed to test the reactions of the defences. Goering had his bombers and fighters fly both singly or in formation, at height or at low level and from all sorts of directions. RAF Kenley was the target of such a raid by a Dornier reconnaissance aircraft on 3 July 1940. The German aircraft not only took some photos, but also scattered some bombs over the airfield, though due to the great height from which they were dropped the aiming was poor and no real damage was done.

Among the RAF pilots sent up to meet these raiders was Sergeant Jack Mann operating out of Kenley with No.64 Squadron. At this date he was relatively inexperienced, being new to the squadron and to combat. All that would change rapidly. One of his first experiences of air combat made a huge impression on him. In a struggle high over southern England one of his flight was badly hit by German bullets. The pilot baled out, but his parachute failed and he fell to his death as Mann watched in horror. Thereafter, Mann decided, he would never bale out.

A few days later, Mann was engaged in a dogfight over the Channel when his Spitfire was hit by 15 cannon shells fired by a Messerschmitt Bf109. The crippled aircraft was clearly doomed, but Mann was determined not to bale out. He nursed the Spitfire towards a distant patch of land. Crash-landing into a field, Mann saw his starboard wing break

A bronze bust of Hermann Goering kept at Bentley Priory,
Dowding's control centre during the Battle of Britain.

off and cartwheel over the turf, killing two sheep. Scrambling from the wreckage, Mann grabbed his parachute and pushed it roughly into a water-filled ditch. He hoped that when the Germans came to inspect the crash they would notice that the parachute was missing and assume that the pilot had baled out over the sea.

With the head start that he hoped this ruse would give him, Mann set off to get as far away from the crash as he could by nightfall. He then planned to follow the guidance given to all airmen. He would find an isolated rural house, watch it for a few hours to make sure no Germans were present and then approach the residents to ask if they could put him in touch with the local resistance group.

Mann did not have the chance to put any of this plan into operation. He had gone only a mile or so when he came around a corner almost to bump into an elderly woman cycling in the opposite direction. Not sure what to do, Mann smiled and waved. The woman stopped, eyed Mann up and down for a moment and then said, 'Hello, young man. Had an accident have you?' He was in Kent.

The fourth time Mann was shot down his parents were sent an urgent telegram telling them that he had been killed and that they should come south to make funeral arrangements. The grief-stricken pair arrived at the hospital to be met by a puzzled nurse who told them that Mann had discharged himself that morning and returned to his squadron.

The sixth time that Mann was shot down, he was not so lucky. In March 1941 his Spitfire was hit when far out over the Channel. The Merlin engine caught fire, but rather than bale out or crash-land in nearby France, Mann opted to try to reach England. He did, but only just, and suffered horrific burns on the way. He was taken to Sir Archibald McIndoe's unit at Queen Victoria Hospital in East Grinstead for pioneering plastic surgery to his burns.

Returning to duty many months later, Mann was put on night-fighters, then became a flying instructor. After the war he left the RAF for a career in civil aviation, becoming a pilot for Middle East Airlines and settling in Lebanon. That is why he was in Beirut on 12 May 1989 when he was kidnapped by a terrorist group calling itself the Union of Palestine Refugees. He was held in terrible conditions, being chained up most of the time and beaten if he showed any signs of resistance, which he did daily. His glasses were broken, leaving him almost blind. He was finally released 2 years 4 months and 13 days after he was kidnapped. He was taken back

The entrance to the 11 Group Bunker at RAF Uxbridge. The steel doors would be closed in the event of an air raid. Beyond them a flight of concrete steps leads deep underground.

Pilots from 501 Squadron, which moved to Kenley in September 1940. Among them is 'Ginger' Lacey, who went on to become one of the highest scoring aces in the Battle of Britain.

*A Hurricane I being re-armed with belts of .303 ammunition
for its eight Browning machine guns.*

to England on an RAF transport to be greeted by a Spitfire doing a victory
roll overhead. He died in 1995.

Meanwhile, in July 1940, everyone was becoming aware that a German
invasion of Britain was increasingly likely. The German blitzkrieg attacks
that had taken place to date in Europe had all begun with dawn assaults
by paratroops and glider-borne units. Bridges, road junctions and airfields
had all been targeted, and it was predicted that the German invasion of
Britain would begin with similar attacks on airfields in southern England.
Airborne troops could move fast and strike without warning, but they
could not bring with them heavy weapons.

To guard against such attacks, Kenley and Croydon were invaded by
teams of construction workers who built brick and concrete pillboxes to
house machine guns, reinforced trenches to hold mortars and infantry,

and gunpits for anti-aircraft guns. At Kenley the existing company of the Queen's Royal Regiment was reinforced with a company of the Scots Guards. The Local Defence Volunteers, later to be renamed the Home Guard, were being organised. These part-time soldiers were poorly armed, but they were quickly integrated into the airfield defence plans, undertaking dawn patrols to watch for parachutists and manning guard posts on key approach roads.

As well as these preparations, other measures were taken. A new strip of concrete road near Kenley showed up from the air as a bold white stripe and was easy to see. It was sprayed with patches of different coloured tar to try to mask it from the air and rob the Luftwaffe of an easy waymarker.

On 12 July Prime Minister Churchill came to Kenley accompanied by Air Vice Marshal Keith Park, commander of 11 Group, to see how the preparations were coming along. After a short, morale-boosting visit the pair left by air to visit other Fighter Command bases.

About this time began a series of German bombing attacks on coastal convoys. These consisted primarily of ships that had crossed the Atlantic and were heading for London, either up the Channel or down the North Sea. They habitually hugged the coast to be close to air cover. The German attacks were designed both to damage the convoys and to draw up RAF fighters into a position where they could be ambushed, or 'bounced' in the contemporary jargon, by larger numbers of Luftwaffe aircraft.

The first convoy battle to involve fighters from Surrey came on 10 July when No.111 Squadron was scrambled from Croydon to intercept a force of bombers attacking a convoy off Folkestone. The battle ended with one Dornier and one Hurricane shot down.

On 14 July No.615 (Surrey) Squadron went up to defend a convoy that was passing through the Straits of Dover. Unknown to the pilots, a BBC radio reporter, Charles Gardener, happened to be in Dover at the time. He recorded a blow-by-blow commentary on the air battle as it raged over the convoy. The recording was broadcast later that day and became an instant classic. Two of the pilots from 615 Squadron were killed in the combat.

On 19 July No.111 Squadron flying out of Croydon went up to tackle an air raid on Dover. The squadron claimed to have shot down five German aircraft, but this was impossible to verify as at least one fell into

Prime Minister Winston Churchill visited RAF Kenley several times during the Battle of Britain and the years that followed. Its position close to the route from his home to Whitehall made it a convenient stopping place.

Supermarine Spitfire

Type: Single-seat fighter
Engines: 1030 hp Rolls Royce Merlin
Wingspan: 36 ft 10 in
Length: 29 ft 11 in
Height: 11 ft 5 in
Weight: Empty 4810 lb
Loaded 5844 lb
Armament: 8 x 0.303 machine guns in wings
Max speed: 355 mph
Ceiling: 31,900 ft
Range: 575 miles
Production: 20,351

When the Spitfire entered service it was immediately recognised as being a revolution in aircraft design. With its all-metal cantilevered monoplane design, retractable undercarriage and eight-gun armament the 'Spit' was the most modern and effective aircraft in the RAF. Pilots recognised its easy handling and superlative combat manoeuvrability and it quickly became the favourite of RAF Fighter Command. However, its sophisticated design made it less easy to maintain than other fighters, so the Spitfire was more often unable to fly than the Hurricane. The figures given above are for the Spitfire Mk I, the standard variant during the Battle of Britain. It was later to be produced in 11 main marks, plus three naval variants dubbed 'Seafires' and was the only pre-war Allied fighter to remain in production to the end of the war.

the sea, and others may have limped back the short distance to France. Such battles continued for the rest of the month with unrelenting savagery.

On the German side of the Channel, Goering and his senior commanders had been laying their plans. They had decided that the best way to secure command of the air over the English Channel and their planned invasion beachheads was to bomb to destruction the RAF airfields in southern

Junkers Ju88

Type: Four crew bomber
Engines: 2 x 1200 hp Junkers
Jumo 211B
Wingspan: 59 ft 11 in
Length: 47 ft 2 in
Height: 15 ft 10 in
Weight: Empty 21,717 lb
Loaded 30,865 lb
Armament: 6 x 7.92 mm machine guns in nose, dorsal and ventral
positions plus 4,400 lb of bombs
Max speed: 292 mph
Ceiling: 26,900 ft
Range: 1696 miles
Production: 7,000

The Junkers Ju88 was designed as a high-speed medium bomber in 1936 and it was this variant of the Ju88 that featured most in the Battle of Britain. This Ju88A was designed to be able to carry a fairly heavy bomb load on conventional level bombing missions, but also to be able to deliver a lighter bomb load when dive-bombing. It entered service with the Luftwaffe in August 1939, but was not used much in the Polish campaign as the crews were still getting used to its handling characteristics. It entered combat on 26 September with an attack on British shipping off the Scottish coast and thereafter was seen in increasingly large numbers over the Western Front. The Ju88 was later produced in a bewilderingly large number of variants and models, totalling 15,000 aircraft in all. There were torpedo bombers, night-fighters, reconnaissance aircraft, maritime patrol bombers, ground attack versions. Production continued right up until the day before the Americans captured the Junkers factory in March 1945.

The Ju88A's first major operation during the Battle of Britain was conducted on 11 August 1940. The type was heavily involved in a host of subsequent daylight raids against RAF airfields and also the nocturnal bombing campaign against London that followed.

Britain. Such attacks would have a twofold purpose. First they would mean that the RAF would be forced to fly to the Channel from north of the Thames Valley, putting them at the same disadvantage in terms of fuel levels and duration that they had suffered over Dunkirk. Secondly the targeting of RAF bases would inevitably draw up the RAF fighters to defend the airfields, and the Germans were confident that their fighters had the edge in aerial combat. The RAF was to be destroyed.

Chapter 4

The Storm Breaks

The men and women of RAF Fighter Command in Surrey noticed the first signs that things were about to change on 12 August 1940. That morning a force of German bombers headed for the old Roman fort at Pevensey on the Sussex coast. Passing over the ruined, ancient walls – which were at the time swarming with workmen installing machine gun nests and artillery positions to fight off the expected German invasion – the bombers attacked a small collection of huts and steel masts a short distance away.

The radar station serving Kenley Sector had been destroyed. The radar was working again by dawn next day, though full repairs took rather longer to effect. Other radar stations were hit the same day. Although the damage was quickly put right, these raids came as a nasty shock to Dowding, the head of RAF Fighter Command.

The development of radar had been carried out in conditions of absolute secrecy, so tight that not even the pilots understood how the controllers knew so precisely where the enemy bombers were flying. And yet here was the Luftwaffe targeting the radar stations as if Goering knew all about them. The worry was that if the Germans knew about radar and how important it was to Fighter Command they might bomb the radar stations at regular intervals, putting them out of action and forcing Fighter Command to adopt a different operational strategy.

Basically, Dowding would be left with two options. He could send up his fighters when German bombers were seen crossing the coast, but this would mean that the bombers would almost always reach their target before they could be intercepted and would only be tackled on their way home. Alternatively, Dowding could send up standing patrols to fly far out to sea and report incoming bombers as they passed by, but this would enormously increase the strain on his men and machines.

Unknown to Dowding or anyone else in RAF Fighter Command, the secret of the radar stations and considerable detail about airfields in Surrey had been betrayed to the Germans by a man living in Kingston, Surrey, who was working for the Abwehr, the German military secret service. Arthur Owens was a Welsh electrical engineer whose considerable professional skills did not bring him a large enough income to be able to afford the women and the social life to which he aspired.

During the early 1930s, Owens earned a bit of extra cash by passing on to British intelligence any information he had picked up about foreign electrical engineering on business trips abroad. It was this that gave him the idea that he could earn considerably more money from the German intelligence services by selling them information he acquired during his work on British military contracts, particularly for the RAF. He began working for the Abwehr in 1937, meeting their agents when he was in Germany on business. He built up a network of around 35 men willing to sell him trade secrets in return for cash – with Owens creaming off a hefty commission.

When war broke out, Owens went straight to the British secret services and told them all about his activities spying for the Germans. He told them that now the two countries were at war he could no longer serve the Germans. He suggested that he should now work as a British spy, passing on such messages as they wanted the Germans to have. The plan was put into effect and Owens now had an income from British intelligence as well as from the Abwehr.

In fact, Owens had gone to the British intelligence because he was convinced that he had been caught out a few months earlier and thought his arrest was imminent. Although he did as the British ordered, he continued to provide the Germans with genuine intelligence as well. It was as part of this package that he told them about radar, and about aircraft numbers at Croydon and Kenley. At this stage of the war a German victory looked likely and Owens wanted to be on the winning side. It was not until 1941 that British intelligence rumbled Owens and threw him into prison. The amount of RAF secrets he had sold to the Germans was never fully discovered, but was clearly immense.

Despite knowing about radar, the Luftwaffe was strangely hesitant about destroying the key masts and installations. At the time Dowding and his staff could not understand this, but after the war it was revealed that the Luftwaffe staff team responsible for deciding which targets should be hit were in the habit of crossing off targets that had been thoroughly bombed and marking the date of the raid. The target would be visited by a reconnaissance aircraft a couple of weeks later to see if it had been repaired, and so needed to be bombed again. For some reason the radar installations slipped through this system and remained crossed off as 'destroyed' long after they had in fact been repaired.

On the two days following the raid on the Pevensey radar station, RAF fighter bases were bombed at Manston, Detling, Eastchurch, Lympne and Middle Wallop. The raids were of moderate strength and scattered.

Several of the raids on targets near the coast were carried out by formations of the dreaded Junkers Ju87 Stuka dive-bomber. This astonishingly accurate bomber had created mayhem in Poland, the Low Countries and France as it pounded military targets to oblivion. However, it was slow and clumsy in the air, making it an easy target for enemy fighters. In earlier campaigns it had not faced modern fighters in any real numbers, but in the Battle of Britain that was now beginning it was faced by Hurricanes and Spitfires, and suffered accordingly.

Pilot Officer John Gibson of 501 Squadron from Croydon bagged a Stuka over Folkestone as his eighth and final German victim. Seconds later Gibson was shot down by a Bf109. He wrestled with the controls of his aircraft to steer it away from the town and so avoid civilian casualties. Not until the Hurricane was down to less than a thousand feet did Gibson bale out. He survived, but his injuries were so severe that he did not fly again.

Then on 15 August the long-anticipated storm broke in full. Goering had designated it to be 'Adler Tag', Eagle Day. The day on which the destruction of the RAF would begin. Those serving with the RAF in Surrey at the time were unaware of this boastful codename, but were soon under no illusions that the Germans meant serious business.

The day was one of brilliant sunshine. German raids in the morning were heavy, but again Surrey was not on the hit list. No.111 Squadron took off from Croydon to intercept a force of Dornier bombers coming in

German dive-bombers wheel overhead as a convoy of ships dodges the falling bombs. This photo was taken in early August 1940 as the attacks on convoys in the English Channel and North Sea reached their peak.

over Dover. The resulting battle saw three Germans shot down, but several of the Hurricanes were badly damaged and had to be removed from duty for repair when they landed.

Among the No.111 Squadron pilots involved was Sergeant Thomas Wallace, who had joined the squadron on 17 July. In the month since he entered combat, Wallace had already shot down six enemy aircraft, with another four damaged by his guns. This time he got separated from his squadron, then spotted a formation of German bombers flying south having finished a raid. Wallace turned to pursue them, but the Germans had a good head start. The bombers pushed on over the coast and out over the Channel. Time slipped by, but slowly Wallace caught up with the enemy formation.

As the French coast loomed into view, Wallace pushed the nose of his Hurricane down and dived to deliver a blistering attack that left one of the Germans with smoke pouring from its engines. Satisfied, Wallace turned north to return to England, and almost at once ran into a formation of six Bf110s coming south in the wake of the bombers. Now it was Wallace's turn to be on the receiving end of a diving attack.

Wallace saw the fighters coming and climbed to meet them head on with his guns blazing. As the fighters closed on each other at high speed, Wallace felt bullets striking his Hurricane. His own gunfire was effective, sending one Messerschmitt crashing down into the sea. Then he was clear and racing for home. Glancing round at his shattered aircraft, Wallace saw the wings and fuselage peppered with holes. The engine and controls were, however, undamaged and he managed to get back to base safely.

At 6 pm the surviving nine Hurricanes of No.111 Squadron were sent up again to head for south-east London to intercept a fresh force of Dorniers that was heading towards the Kent fighter station of Biggin Hill. It was 6.30 pm when the lookouts at Croydon airfield saw what they took to be a flight of Blenheim 1F fighters approaching from the north-east. It was not until the bombs began falling and exploding that anyone realised that the 'Blenheims' were in fact Messerschmitt Bf110 fighter-bombers, escorted by a small force of Messerschmitt Bf109 fighters. Men raced to the anti-aircraft guns, while others dived for cover in air raid shelters. Frantic radio messages were sent to the Hurricanes of No.111 Squadron to return to defend their home base.

The Germans delivered their attack as they dived down to gain speed for their escape southward. The bombs fell over a wide area, spreading

*A Hurricane IIC, which now serves with the Battle of Britain Memorial Flight.
The first examples came with a two-bladed propeller, but by 1940 most had a
three-bladed, variable-pitch propeller that greatly enhanced performance.*

destruction not only over the airbase but also over adjacent areas. The Redwing Aircraft Factory was utterly destroyed. A bomb struck a nearby factory just as a meeting of the Board of Directors was beginning – every single director of the company was killed outright. A soap factory was flattened. Houses in Crowley Crescent, Coldharbour Way and Waddon Way were destroyed. On the airbase itself the Officers' Mess was demolished, as were one of the hangars, the armoury and several aircraft. Many other buildings and aircraft were damaged.

In all six men were killed on RAF Croydon and dozens more wounded. The casualty list was longer for civilians with 62 dead and 200 wounded.

As the dark clouds of choking smoke rolled up from the shattered Croydon airfield, the nine Hurricanes of No.111 Squadron were racing to

A German pilot shot down in August 1940 is given a restorative drink by the soldiers who have captured him while a policeman looks on. Many German aircrew had been told that they would be tortured to reveal information and were pleasantly surprised by the reception they received.

the rescue. They arrived too late to interrupt the raid, but caught up with the Germans over Redhill. The German twin-engine aircraft adopted their regulation spinning circle formation in which the rear gun of each covered the following aircraft while its forward-firing cannon protected that in front. The Germans climbed for height, knowing that once they put their noses down and raced south they would soon outpace the Hurricanes.

One Messerschmitt Bf110 did not make it. The aircraft piloted by Horst Fiedler was shot at by the Hurricane piloted by Sergeant Dymond. The port engine exploded and the aircraft fell out of the sky and crashed on the edge of Redhill airfield. Fiedler was killed in the crash, but his gunner Johann Werner managed to bale out. As he floated down to earth on his parachute, Werner was watched by a company of the West Nova Scotia Regiment, a Canadian unit which was on manoeuvres in the area training to meet the expected German invasion. The men had got their bayonets fixed even before their captain gave the order to race after the parachute as it drifted by. The Canadians kept pace with the drifting airman and welcomed Werner to England with levelled bayonets and the offer of a cigarette. Werner accepted the cigarette and sat patiently oblivious to the ribald remarks of his captors until an ambulance arrived to take him off to hospital to have his minor wounds dealt with. The delighted Canadians divided up the German parachute as souvenirs to post back home and jubilantly entered into the regiment's official diary their first prisoner taken.

Meanwhile, the battle raged overhead. Then the Germans broke for home, pursued by the Hurricanes. Flight Lieutenant Connors shot down a Bf110 over Horley, while pilots arriving from Kent shot down four more Bf110s and a Bf109. The pilots of No.111 Squadron returned to Croydon without loss to find the place a shambles. The ground teams set to work to clear the debris and repair the damage. By noon next day Croydon was functioning again, after a fashion, but it was several days before the damage was repaired completely. The pilots of No.111 Squadron were back in the air by 3 pm, sent to intercept 200 Dorniers droning in over Dungeness. They shot down four German aircraft, for the loss of one Hurricane.

The next day saw bad weather and little in the way of German raids. Sunday 18 August dawned bright and clear, but the morning passed with little fighting. At 12.45 pm RAF Kenley received orders from Group to scramble the Hurricanes of No.615 Squadron. Ten minutes later the

A Hurricane MkI on the ground after returning from combat. The muzzles of the machine guns can be clearly seen. These would usually be covered by a protective screen of fabric, that was shot away as the first bullets emerged.

Spitfires of No.64 Squadron were ordered up, though only eight of them got airborne as the rest were under repair. At 1.05 pm No.111 Squadron at Croydon was ordered into the air.

The cause of the rush to get fighters into the air was a force of around 60 German bombers that had been picked up by radar climbing for height as they cruised north over the English Channel heading for the Beachy Head area. Watching the markers moving over the map in the Kenley operations room was Wing Commander Thomas Prickman, the station commander. It looked as if the raid was heading for Biggin Hill in Kent, but he was not a man to take chances. Prickman ordered Kenley to go to action stations and prepare for a raid. For some reason the message was not passed to the civilian authorities but an air raid warden living near the base heard the sirens blare. Leaping on his bike, Warden Stephen Reid raced around Kenley blowing his whistle and shouting at people to take cover.

At 1.10 pm a new marker suddenly appeared on the map as an Observer Corps post phoned in to report a startling new development. Nine Dornier bombers were racing north over Bletchingley at a height of under 50 ft. They had come in under the radar cover and had not been detected. They were heading straight for Kenley. Prickman hurriedly ordered every available aircraft into the sky. Those able to fight had to climb for height, those in no fit condition were to head north away from the rapidly approaching danger.

The Dornier Do217 was introduced in 1941 to replace the Do17.
The new bomber was larger, faster and able to carry four times
as many bombs as its predecessor.

At Kenley the retired Major Marshall had heard Warden Reid's whistle and was walking towards the air raid shelter when he heard the sudden roar of aircraft engines approaching at low level. He turned to see the Dorniers appearing over a line of trees and at that instant received a bullet through his leg. He was the first casualty of the day. He would not be the last.

Seconds later Mr Whittaker of the Auxiliary Fire Service was leaving his fire station when he heard air engines and looked up to see the nine Dorniers approaching. He threw himself flat as a spray of bullets tore up the concrete around him. Six ambulances parked outside the fire station were destroyed. A bomb destroyed three houses in Oak Road and killed a resident, Mrs Charlton. The milkman outside managed to dive for cover, but his horse was killed in the blast.

Unknown to the hapless civilians on the ground, the fast-approaching Dorniers were from the specialist 9 Staffel (squadron) of the 76 Kammpfgeshwader led by Hauptmann Joachim Roth. This squadron was specially trained in low-level flying and bombing, for just this sort of raid.

A Spitfire pilot gives a comrade the thumbs up signal as he prepares to leave on patrol in August 1940. The pressure under which Fighter Command was operating at this time can be seen from the gun blast streaks under the wings. Ground crews would normally have removed these before the aircraft left for combat.

They had studied aerial photos of Kenley and now picked out their allotted targets as they raced in over the airfield perimeter. In addition to their usual bombs and machine guns these low-level attackers had a deadly 20 mm cannon in the nose to destroy vehicles and aircraft on the ground. The bombs too were adapted for low-level attack, having fuses that set them off a few seconds after impact to give the aircraft time to get away from the blast.

On the runway a Hurricane piloted by Pilot Officer Lofts was racing to get airborne. Seeing the German aircraft, Lofts threw his aircraft into a screaming turn as soon as he was airborne and then climbed for height. The bombs began to fall, destroying three hangars with wooden roofs. Amazingly Corporal Storry, who was manning an anti-aircraft gun on the brick pillar of one of these hangars, continued to fire at the raiders even as the wooden roof of the hangar was blown upward. One of the Dorniers mistimed its run and was thrown upward around 200 ft by the blast of a bomb dropped by the aircraft ahead of it. The runway was blasted by several bombs, as was the main taxiway. Cannon fire tore into parked aircraft, destroying eight of them. Nine men were killed on the ground.

But RAF Kenley had a nasty surprise in store for the raiders. Sitting in a trench on the edge of the airfield was Aircraftman Roberts. He was in charge of firing a fan of rockets, each of which trailed behind it a steel cable. The rockets were designed to drag the cable up to a height of several thousand feet, then deploy a parachute so that the cable remained suspended for some seconds. Any aircraft that hit the cables, it was thought, would be dragged down by the sheer weight of metal. Timing was crucial: release too early and the cable would be lying uselessly on the ground when the aircraft passed over, fire too late and the cables would not deploy properly.

Roberts sat alone, calmly watching the carnage unfolding in front of his eyes and trying to calculate the speed of the approaching bombers. When he thought the moment right he pushed the firing button. The rockets roared up, dragging their cables behind them. One Dornier clipped a

The graves in Whyteleafe Cemetery of the RAF personnel killed during the heavy German air raid on the fighter base that took place on 18 August 1940. This day saw the heaviest air fighting over Surrey of the entire Battle of Britain.

The crashed Dornier flown by Joachim Roth, following the attack on Kenley.

cable, lurched sideways, then raced on apparently unscathed. A second bomber hit the cables full on, spun and crashed in a vast ball of orange flame that licked over the trench as Roberts dived for cover.

At the North Gate, the company of Scots Guards were deployed. Lance Corporal J. Miller was manning the anti-aircraft gun and kept firing as a Dornier flew straight at him. The Dornier released a bomb which scored a direct hit on Miller and his gun, both of which disappeared in the blast. Miller's death was not entirely in vain. The Dornier flown by Joachim Roth was badly hit and crashed some miles away on its run for home.

Meanwhile, a flight of Hurricanes belonging to No.111 Squadron from Croydon had arrived and were diving down into the fray. Pilot Officer James Simpson hit one of the rocket cables, but got his aircraft down safely on the Woodcote Golf Course just outside Epsom. A group of golfers dived for cover as the Hurricane skidded on its belly over the fairway. Then they raced to help Simpson, who had been wounded in the foot. The golf club stood Simpson a fine lunch and plenty of liquid refreshment before a member drove him back to Croydon.

Sergeant Harry Newton got on the tail of a Dornier and closed to firing range as the aircraft raced low over Woldingham. The two aircraft opened

Squadron Leader Peter Townsend, shown here with pilots of 85 Squadron, returning to Croydon after he had been shot down at the end of August in 1940. 85 Squadron had replaced the hard pressed 111 Squadron at Croydon in mid-August.

fire at the same instant, but it was the Hurricane which went down. Newton baled out and was astonished when his parachute opened in time despite the lack of height. He was arrested by a squad of Scots Guards with fixed bayonets, but was quickly released to the care of an ambulance driver.

Another pilot of No.111 Squadron to go down was Sgt. Harry Deacon. He had gone through the campaign in France and had returned to duty only 23 hours earlier. He went after the Dorniers, but was badly wounded in one leg by return fire and broke off the pursuit to return to Croydon. He was flying back over Kenley, holding a pad to his wounded leg, when the anti-aircraft gunners at Kenley opened up having mistaken his Hurricane for a Messerschmitt Bf109. Sadly their aim was good and Deacon's starboard wing was blown off. He baled out and came down safely.

Meanwhile the high-level raid that had been heading toward RAF Biggin Hill had swung west and was now also heading for RAF Kenley. The force consisted of 27 Dornier Do17 and 12 Junkers Ju88 bombers plus 20 Messerschmitt Bf110 twin-engine bombers. Flying high above them waiting to bounce any RAF fighters that came to attack were 60 Messerschmitt Bf109 fighters. It was a formidable formation.

The Hurricanes of No.32 Squadron and No.615 Squadron were racing to intercept, but the pilots did not spot the 109s high above. The Germans dived down out of the sun to take No.615 Squadron from behind. Three Hurricanes went down almost at once, but the rest turned on their attackers and a dogfight developed.

Pilot Officer David Looker was one of those whose Hurricane was riddled with bullets in the first encounter. He crash-landed on Croydon airfield, suffered concussion in doing so and spent some weeks in hospital. Looker's Hurricane was later repaired, survived the war and is now on display at London's Science Museum.

A second pilot to have his fighter hit was Pilot Officer Petrus 'Dutch' Hugo, who already had five confirmed kills to his name. His engine was knocked out and he spun out of control for 22,000 ft before he managed to get his Hurricane under control, but was then attacked by a Bf109 that had followed him down. Hugo was hit badly, the inside of his cockpit canopy being so covered in blood that he could not see out of it. He tried to bale out, but his seat straps would not release so he went down for a crash-landing. The Bf109 was still attacking as he belly-landed in a field. He skidded to a halt, then scrambled out and fled for cover. A few minutes later an ambulance crew arrived to take him away. He was found to have a bullet in one leg and numerous shrapnel wounds to head and chest.

That marked the end of Hugo's career in the Battle of Britain, but not in the war. He was back with No.615 Squadron as a Flight Lieutenant in September 1941 in time to take part in offensive sweeps over northern France and to escort bombers attacking German shipping. He went down to strafe two E-boats, badly damaging both of them. He also shot up an oil plant, causing one huge storage tank to explode with a shattering blast. During this phase of his career Hugo got a fifth confirmed kill.

After a spell of non-flying duties, Hugo was promoted to Wing Commander and sent to North Africa with No.322 Wing. By February 1943 he had shot down four more enemy aircraft and had 'displayed gallant leadership and great skill during an outstanding record of operational flying'. He ended the war with a DSO and two bars to his DFC.

The third pilot of No.615 to go down was Sergeant Kenneth Walley. He had not been due to fly on 18 August, but took to the air in a reserve Hurricane as the Germans thundered in. Walley regained control of his aircraft as it dived down over Merton, then over St Helier. Suddenly the engine cut out and the Hurricane began to go down, heading for houses in London Road. Watchers on the ground saw the aircraft turn aside from the houses, heading for a nearby field but it did not make it and crashed in flames into woodland. Walley was killed instantly. Those who had seen the crash were convinced that he gave his life trying to avoid the civilian casualties that would have followed if his aircraft had hit the houses.

No.32 Squadron had meanwhile found themselves flying head on at the German bombers. The Bf110 heavy fighters were seen coming down and one flight of Hurricanes soared up to meet them. The rest of the Hurricanes pushed on toward the bombers, closing with them at the nerve-rackingly high speed of eight miles a minute. Only one German was shot down in this initial run, but the formation was broken up. With RAF fighters weaving and diving around them, and their own aircraft taking evasive action, some of the German bomb-aimers found it impossible to aim straight. Their bombs fell over a wide area around Kenley, only a few hitting the airfield. Two of the bombers mistook Croydon for Kenley and bombed that base instead. Others pushed on to Kenley and dropped their bombs accurately.

Air Raid Warden Reid was pedalling like mad back toward his post when the high-level bombers arrived. A bomb exploded only 10 yards away from him, knocking him to the ground though he was uninjured except for minor scrapes. He later went to investigate the crashed Dornier brought down by the rocket wires. He helped drag the dead German crew from the wreck, noticing as he did so that one had a large hole worn in the sole of his boot. He later recorded thinking, 'You think you are the Master Race, but you wear worn out boots.'

The damage to Kenley was extensive. The Operations Building had escaped a direct hit, but all the phone lines except one were cut, the roof was covered by debris and the windows smashed. An air raid shelter had received a direct hit at its entrance, killing those nearby and entombing the rest. It took some time to release the trapped men and women, several of whom were wounded. Among the nine dead was Kenley's enormously popular medical officer, 'Doc' Crombie, killed when a bomb hit the hospital block. His place was taken by the village doctor, Dr Lewis, who walked onto the base a few minutes after the raid to set up a temporary medical post in the only hangar still standing.

The airbase was out of action and the returning fighters were diverted to land at RAF Redhill instead. The work of clearing up began next morning as contractors moved in to bulldoze rubble into craters and repair the runway and taxiways. It took weeks until the airbase was back to normal, but it was back in operation the next day.

That was the day that the Spitfires of No.616 Squadron arrived at Kenley. The feelings of the pilots, brought down from a relatively quiet sector in Yorkshire, on seeing their new base a mass of rubble and burned out vehicles can be best imagined. Among the pilots arriving with No.616 was a 20-year-old Hugh Dundas who, despite his tender years, was already a veteran with a forceful reputation as an air fighter.

Dundas had been found a position with a solicitor by his parents, but at the age of 18 volunteered to join the RAF. He failed the medical, spent some weeks building himself up and then failed it again. The third failure of the medical test almost saw Dundas go back to his career as a lawyer but in May 1939 the gathering clouds of war had persuaded the RAF to overlook his minor fitness problems in favour of his other talents. He trained as a fighter pilot and joined No.616 Squadron. He entered combat in May 1940 over the war-torn beaches of Dunkirk and found the experience both terrifying and confusing.

After Dunkirk No.616 went to RAF Leaconfield in Yorkshire. On 15 August, as Croydon was being bombed, Dundas was shooting down a Junkers Ju88 bomber over the North Sea as his squadron tangled with a large formation of incoming German aircraft. He also damaged a second bomber which was subsequently finished off by another pilot.

The day after their arrival at Kenley, No.616 was put on standby immediately after breakfast and remained sitting close to their Spitfires awaiting the scramble signal for the rest of the day. Bad weather had persuaded the Luftwaffe to scale back their attacks and the squadron was not needed. That did nothing to calm the gnawing anxiety of being always ready for instant action, but never being called upon. The next day the same thing happened, though the Spitfires were sent up once only to be called back again when the incoming German formation turned for home.

On 22 August they again spent the whole day sitting around at constant readiness, but without seeing any action. At 4 pm the pilots were told that they could stand down and would not be needed again until next morning. With some jubilation the pilots grabbed tea then dashed to their rooms to change into their best uniforms for a night on the town up in London.

At 5 pm a car pulled up at the front gates of RAF Kenley. The guard on duty stepped forward to see who it was, then snapped smartly to attention and sent an urgent message to Wing Commander Prickman telling him to get to the front gate immediately. The car contained Winston Churchill who was returning to London from a visit elsewhere and had decided to drop in on Kenley to see how things were going and give a boost to morale at the stricken airfield.

Prickman at once ordered No.616 Squadron back to readiness, causing the cursing pilots to run back to their dispersal hut, retrieve parachutes and flying kit and get their Spitfires ready for take off. Churchill came out to the dispersal hut to shake hands with all the pilots, stopping to have a little chat with each before moving on to tour the rest of the airfield. Seconds later the scramble bell rang and the Spitfires of No.616 raced to get into the air.

Dundas, at least, thought the scramble had been staged for Churchill's benefit, but he was wrong. A new raid of Germans was coming in over Dover and No.616 was sent to intercept. What the radar had not detected, and the pilots of No.616 did not see was that an escort of Bf109s was cruising high above the bombers waiting to pounce on any British fighters that tried to intervene. And No.616 flew straight into the trap.

The first anybody knew of the Messerschmitts was when a hail of cannon shells tore into Dundas's Spitfire. The engine caught fire, the fuselage and wings were riddled with splinters and the aircraft dropped into a deadly spin. Dundas began to bale out, but the canopy jammed when it was only an inch open. He then wrestled with the controls to try

A pilot dozes in a chair at dispersal. He has on his flying jacket and flying boots indicating that he is at readiness. Were combat considered imminent he would be in his fighter with the engine running.

Aircrew play a game of draughts at dispersal while awaiting the order to scramble. Some days pilots would spend hours waiting, other days they would be almost constantly in the air.

to pull out of the spin, but to no avail. His Spitfire was too badly damaged. With the ground rapidly approaching, Dundas gave the canopy a final, despairing tug and felt it give way.

Clambering up, Dundas found himself jammed against the side of the cockpit by the centrifugal forces of the vicious spin. It took great effort to get out of the cockpit to slither along the fuselage and finally fall free. As he hit clear air he pulled his parachute ripcord. The parachute opened and he found himself floating gently. Looking down, Dundas saw his Spitfire hit the ground and explode, causing a flock of sheep to bolt in terror. He hit the ground 300 yards from the wreckage with a dislocated shoulder and a horrible leg wound. The farmer who owned the sheep came over, covering Dundas with a shotgun in case he turned out to be a German. A few minutes later a Home Guard unit arrived. They had seen the Spitfire go down and wanted to buy the downed pilot a drink.

A squadron scramble bell as preserved at RAF Bentley Priory, Dowding's former HQ. The writing on the bell reads 'Ring the Bell and run like "Hell" '. In 2008 it was serving as the time bell at the officers' bar.

Then an army patrol turned up and sent for an ambulance on the grounds that the wounded Dundas was in no condition for a trip to the village pub.

Dundas did not return to No.616 Squadron until the autumn, by which time the squadron had moved to Duxford in East Anglia. When spring 1941 came Dundas enthusiastically joined the offensive sweeps over northern France. One such mission saw him over Calais when his engine received a stream of bullets and packed up. Turning for England, Dundas managed to glide right across the Channel and then land in a field.

Dundas later spent some time training Free French pilots before being given command of a squadron of the new Hawker Typhoons. He led the squadron to France in August 1942 to help cover the disastrous Dieppe raid during which so many Canadians lost their lives. He later transferred to the Italian front, where he was shot down again and promoted to

A formation of Spitfire MkI fighters in the air over England. The positioning of the guns on the wings was dictated by the complex interior structure of the elliptical wing frame.

Group Captain – the youngest man to achieve the rank. After the war he went into business, eventually rising to be Chairman of Thames Television in the 1980s and doing much to prepare the way for the boom in cable TV that followed his retirement. After retiring, Dundas worked for both the RAF Benevolent Fund and the Macmillan Cancer Relief Fund. He was knighted in 1987 and died in 1995.

The days after Dundas was shot down saw bad weather, but the Luftwaffe returned to Surrey skies on 30 August, the day that a new squadron, No.253, arrived at Kenley. The men of the squadron were still unpacking when the scramble alarm sounded and 13 Hurricanes went up to face a formation of bombers heading north over Kent, apparently heading for Farnborough.

The Hurricanes pounced on the bombers, which turned out to be Heinkel He111s, near Lingfield. Pilot Officer John Greenwood – a Surrey man having been born in Richmond – got behind one of the bombers and managed to pour in an accurate stream of bullets. The bomber lurched then dived down to crash-land in a field belonging to Haxted Farm. Greenwood swooped down low enough to see the crew clambering out, then climbed back up toward the continuing battle. Pilot Officer Novak also shot up a bomber, but although he saw it diving apparently out of control it did not crash and is thought to have staggered back to France.

Meanwhile the bombers' escort of Messerschmitt Bf109 fighters had come down to join the fray. Two of the Messerschmitts were brought down, but they took their toll on the Hurricanes they faced.

Another Surrey pilot, Pilot Officer Colin Francis of Stoke D'Abernon, was one of the first to be shot down. Neither he nor his aircraft were discovered until the wreckage was found deep in a wood in 1980. His body was recovered and given a decent funeral.

Also killed was Pilot Officer David Jenkins, and his death quickly became notorious. He was seen baling out safely, but when his parachute was found it was attached to his body that was riddled with German bullets. It was assumed that some Messerschmitt pilot had deliberately killed him as he hung helpless in his parachute harness. The event, not surprisingly, led to a lot of ill-feeling in No.253 Squadron.

The aerial combat was interesting for other reasons. Both sides mistook the aircraft against which they were fighting. The aircrew of the Heinkel He111 brought down by Greenwood in his Hurricane were convinced that they had been shot down by a Spitfire. Meanwhile, Pilot Officer Novak reported that the Heinkel he had damaged was a Junkers Ju86.

The Junkers Ju86 was one of the less numerous bombers in the Luftwaffe with only 450 being built in all. It was designed in 1936 and identified by the RAF as a partner to the Ju88, though its precise role and abilities were unclear. In fact the Ju86 was designed more as a high-altitude reconnaissance aircraft able to carry a few bombs rather than as a bomber. It was able to fly at the then astonishing height of 46,000 ft for 1000 miles. None of these aircraft was airborne on 30 August.

The Luftwaffe came back next day, and it proved to be a bad day for the Hurricanes. The target this time was RAF Croydon, the Heinkel He111 bombers somehow managing to mislead the Observer Corps as to their destination until the last minute. As a result the Hurricanes of No.85 Squadron that were on the ground did not get the order to scramble until moments before the bombing began. Several fighters, including that flown by Squadron Leader Peter Townsend, were still racing over the airfield to get into the air as the bombs fell.

Townsend was later to become rather better known for his romance with Princess Margaret than for his wartime heroics, but they were impressive enough. He had joined the RAF in 1935 and proved to be such a skilled pilot that he was posted to the prestigious No.1 Squadron of Fighter Command. After a time in Singapore on bombers, Townsend returned to fly fighters in September 1938 and never flew anything else again.

His war began flying out of Northumberland where he got his first kill, a Heinkel bomber that crashed near Whitby. Townsend later visited the German survivors in hospital and was to become a post-war friend of the pilot, Karl Missy. He then moved to Scotland to defend the naval base at Scapa Flow and gained two more victims. In July 1940 he was himself shot down over the North Sea and baled out to splash down in the chill waters. It was only by luck that the crew of a minesweeper saw his parachute and rescued him.

On this particular August day over Surrey, Townsend was to be unlucky again. His Hurricane was bounced by a Messerschmitt and riddled with cannon shells. One of the exploding shells sent a red hot splinter deep into Townsend's left foot. As the aircraft began to break up, Townsend baled out and found himself floating down to land in a garden in Goudhurst. He was out of action for a month and by the time he returned to his squadron it was to find that 14 of the 18 pilots had been shot down.

A formation of Heinkel He111 bombers heading towards England. These are the more advanced model He111H, which entered service in 1939 and made up 6,200 of the 7,300 He111 bombers built.

In June 1941 he was taken off combat duty for a while and married. His subsequent promotion to the staff job of Officer Commanding Night Operations, caused a fair amount of ribaldry among his colleagues. In December 1942 Townsend returned to combat duties at West Malling, Kent, but a sudden and severe illness put him back in a ground-based job – this time permanently. He had shot down a confirmed 11 German aircraft.

It was in 1944 that he was transferred to be equerry to King George VI. By 1952 when King George died, Townsend realised that he was in love with Princess Margaret and she returned his feelings. However, it was impossible in the 1950s for a princess to marry a divorced commoner, so the romance was broken off. Townsend left the RAF for a career in journalism. He remarried in 1959 and later moved to France. He died in 1995.

Townsend was not the only fighter pilot flying out of Surrey to be shot down on 31 August 1940. No.253 Squadron had taken off from Kenley to tackle a force of bombers attacking Biggin Hill. During the ensuing

Squadron Leader Peter Townsend led his No.85 Squadron into Croydon in mid-August 1940. Within two weeks, 14 of the 18 pilots had been shot down and Townsend himself was in hospital.

combat, Squadron Leader Gleave was attacked by a Messerschmitt Bf109 and shot down in flames. His burns were so severe that he did not return to flying duties. Pilot Officer Alec Trueman was also shot down, but he managed to get out of his stricken Hurricane in one piece.

No.79 Squadron was also in action. Pilot Officer George Nelson-Edwards bagged a 109 but was almost immediately shot down himself over Limpsfield. He suffered minor leg injuries but was quickly back in action with his squadron. Exactly what happened to Sergeant Henry Bolton at just past 1 pm over Woldingham is not clear. His Hurricane was seen diving down in obvious trouble, levelled out, rose to clear a row of trees then suddenly fell out of the sky. A Mr Fuller ran to help to find the pilot, Bolton, sitting in the wreck of the cockpit. Fuller tried to pull Bolton free, but the pilot lost consciousness and died in Fuller's arms. It was later found that Bolton had a bullet wound in his back. Seven hours later some revenge was gained when a Bf109 was shot down over Tandridge by Polish pilots of No.303 Squadron.

August had been a bloody month for Fighter Command in Surrey. September promised to be even worse as the long-feared German invasion was due to become a reality.

Heinkel He111

Type:	Five crew medium bomber
Engines:	2 x 1200 hp Junkers Jumo 211D-1
Wingspan:	74 ft 1 in
Length:	53 ft 9 in
Height:	13 ft 1 in
Weight:	Empty 17,000 lb Loaded 30,865 lb
Armament:	1 x 20 mm cannon in nose, 1 x 13 mm machine gun in dorsal position, 7 x 7.9 mm machine guns in ventral, beam and nose positions.
Bomb load:	7165 lb
Max speed:	252 mph
Ceiling:	21,980 ft
Range:	1280 miles
Production:	7,300

The figures given above are for the Heinkel He111H, of which over 6,000 were built. There were 11 other models, one of them a naval torpedo bomber, but these were built in only small numbers. The H was the sixth model in the series and the first to have the distinctive glazed nose. The 111 first entered service in 1936, the H model arriving in 1939. It was the mainstay of the Luftwaffe's bombing arm and was classified as a heavy bomber when it first appeared, though it is now generally reckoned a medium bomber in comparison to the Allied four-engine giants that appeared later in the war. The Luftwaffe remained primarily dedicated to helping the army by bombing military targets behind the front lines, plus the occasional terror raid, such as those on Warsaw and Rotterdam, to bully an enemy government into early surrender. In such roles the Heinkel He111 was supreme. Five Kampfgeschwader and one Kampfgruppe were equipped with He111s during the Battle of Britain, operating from seven bases in France and one in Norway, with the first major operation involving the type (72 He111H-4s) taking place on 15 August 1940. Daylight operations gave way to nocturnal attacks in mid-September 1940.

Junkers Ju87 'Stuka'

Type: Two seat dive-bomber
Engine: 1x 1100hp Junkers Jumo 211Da
Wingspan: 45 ft 3 in
Length: 36 ft 5 in
Height: 13 ft 2 in
Weight: Empty 5,980 lb
                 Loaded 9369 lb
Armament: 2 x 7.92 mm machine guns in wings
                 plus 1 x 7.92 mm machine gun in rear of cockpit
Bomb load: 1540 lb
Max speed: 211 mph
Ceiling: 26,150 ft
Range: 490 miles
Production: 5709

The Stuka, short for 'sturzkampfflugzeug', 'diving-war-flying-weapon', was the most famous and effective of all the dive-bombers produced during the war. Ironically Junkers began development of the Stuka with a Rolls Royce engine, converting to the Jumo when war with Britain seemed imminent. The terror induced by the Stuka for its victims on the ground was due in part to the phenomenal accuracy with which it could drop its main 500 kg bomb, but was enhanced by the addition of a wind-powered siren fixed to the legs which emitted a distinctive and very loud wailing scream as the aircraft dived to deliver its bomb load. It was withdrawn from the Battle of Britain early on as losses mounted, but went on to play a key role in the German invasion of Russia. A specialised anti-shipping variant, the Ju87R, had extra fuel tanks to increase its range.

By 20 July 1940, 316 Ju87Bs and Ju87Rs were available for use against Great Britain in seven Stukagruppen. The type's first major operation in strength during the Battle of Britain was on 8 August 1940; the last involving Stukas in any significant numbers came just ten days later with an attack on RAF bases at Thorney Island and Ford, during which sixteen Ju87B-1s were lost.

Chapter 5

The Eye
of the
Storm

By the end of August 1940 the Battle of Britain was approaching crisis point, and both the Luftwaffe and RAF were showing signs of serious strain. Losses were mounting, morale was suffering and tiredness was setting in. That was just among the front line units. Further up the chain of command both sides were suffering from internal disputes that threatened to disrupt the effort and paralyse the organisation.

On the German side, the dispute was largely between the bomber commanders and the fighter commanders. Goering, a fighter pilot during the First World War, was forced to find a solution to the arguments. The underlying problem was the high rate of casualties among the bombers during raids on RAF Fighter Command stations which had mostly been caused by Hurricanes and Spitfires getting into a good attacking position before they had been spotted by the German aircrew. The attacks had been delivered at high speed and, mostly, were over in seconds with the RAF fighters diving away without turning back to renew the assault.

The German air crew did not realise that the British fighters were able to adopt these tactics because of radar. The fighters could get into a good

A pair of Bf109 fighters prepare for take off on an airfield in northern France. The square-tipped wings of the Bf109 were a distinctive feature of models up to and including the Bf109E. Around 4,000 of these fighters were produced by the Messerschmitt company.

position while still out of sight of the German formations as they had been guided there by radar. Nor did they need to stay and dogfight as they knew that they or another squadron would be vectored in by radar to launch a new attack.

These tactics meant that the Messerschmitt Bf109 fighters that were usually positioned several thousand feet above the bombers had little chance to intervene. The tactic of having a high-altitude escort relied for its success on the enemy fighters making two or more passes on the bomber formation to give the Bf109s time to drop down with the advantage of height and speed.

At first the Germans countered by putting units of Messerschmitt Bf110 twin-engine fighters close in alongside the bombers. The Bf110 was heavily armed with two 20 mm cannon and five machine guns – giving it a greater hitting power than the Bf109 with its two 20 mm cannon and two machine guns. And with one machine gun in the rear of the cockpit able to be swung from side to side by the navigator/gunner, the Bf110

A quartet of Bf110Cs fly in formation. The Bf110 was nicknamed the Zerstörer, the 'Destroyer', by its Luftwaffe crews due to its heavy armament of two cannon and five machine guns.

could shoot sideways and upwards as well as forward. However, the Bf110 was 30 mph slower than the Hurricane and 60 mph slower than the Spitfire, and could be out turned by both in a dogfight. They were something of a deterrent to the RAF, but not much.

Thus by the end of August the Luftwaffe bomber commanders were demanding that they had close escorts composed exclusively of Bf109 fighters. Only by keeping the nimble Bf109s near the bombers would they be in a position to intervene in the sort of hit and run attacks the RAF was favouring.

The German fighter commanders were appalled by the idea. They pointed out that for the Bf109s to fly close escort would hand the RAF a double advantage. First it would give the RAF the advantage of height and speed over the Bf109s. Second, once the RAF pilots realised that there was no high-altitude escort they would take their time about forming up for the attack, making each assault all the more effective.

As a fighter pilot of great success himself, Goering knew that his fighter commanders were correct. But he also knew that he could not afford to continue losing bombers at the rate he had been. His answer was a reorganisation of deployment and change of tactics.

The Bf109 units were concentrated around Calais, where they were closer to Britain. Bombers flying from Normandy would be escorted only by Bf110s. This would make them more vulnerable to attack, but in recompense they were sent against only coastal targets by day. Targets further inland were to be attacked at night. Meanwhile, bombers flying from bases around Calais would be given a double escort of Bf109 fighters – made possible by the increase in numbers based locally. There would be a close escort and a high altitude escort. That way Goering hoped to give the bombers what they needed, while still allowing the Bf109 fighter pilots in the high-altitude escort the freedom they needed to bounce the RAF fighters and inflict losses.

And if German combat air crew did not know about British radar, Goering and his senior commanders did – though they were at this point rather hazy as to its precise capabilities. They decided to use the RAF's own radar to give themselves an advantage.

The first move was to form specialist forces of Bf110 twin-engine fighters. Their task was to fly in formations and on courses as if they were bombers. They would cross the Channel, fly a few miles over British territory, then turn and dive fast back toward France. The idea was to fool

A reconnaissance photo of Boulogne harbour taken by the RAF in August 1940.
The barges and other craft assembled by the Germans for the
invasion of Britain can be clearly seen.

the British radar into thinking these formations really were bombers. The RAF fighters would go up to intercept, but would find nothing except Bf110s flying off at speed. Goering hoped that the RAF pilots would become worn out by the many fruitless scrambles – and indeed tiredness did rapidly become a problem.

The Luftwaffe also brought large numbers of transport aircraft and obsolete types to northern France. When a raid was due to head for Britain, these aircraft would take off and mill around over their air bases as if they were bombers getting ready to form up. The British radar, it was hoped, would be unable to distinguish between the real bombers and the decoys. The controllers would delay scrambling the fighters until they were certain which was the real raid, giving the bombers a better chance of evading the RAF fighters altogether.

Finally, the Germans realised that the radar was much more reliable off the coast than over land – where in fact radar did not work at all. To take advantage of this the Germans began sending all their bombers across the Channel in one vast formation, which then broke up once over land as the bombers peeled off to head for their individual targets. This, it was hoped, would also mislead the RAF controllers as to where the bombers were heading and so where the fighters should be sent to intercept them.

The German tactics were a huge success. German losses fell dramatically and RAF losses rose. Just as important, considerably more German bombers got through to their targets unmolested and were able to bomb with accuracy.

A minor, but still significant, success for the Luftwaffe at this period was the arrival of the Heinkel He113 high-altitude fighter. This fighter was heavily armed, with a single 30 mm cannon and two heavy machine guns, and was fast at around 380 mph. News of the fighter first leaked out via journalists from neutral countries who spotted the aircraft during a visit to a Luftwaffe base, but Goering later proudly showed off the fighter in a demonstration to the world's press just as the Battle of Britain was getting under way.

In fact the He113 was a bluff. There were only about half a dozen prototypes in existence, those that had been shown to the journalists. This did not stop the Germans from exploiting British wariness about this high-altitude, high-speed fighter. They stripped down a few Bf109 fighters to improve their height and speed at the cost of guns and armour. These aircraft were sent up to take position well above the upper escort of the

The Heinkel He113 high-speed fighter was an elaborate bluff. The Luftwaffe managed to convince the RAF that hundreds of these heavily-armed fighters were about to enter service in September 1940.

bomber formation in the hope that British fighters would take them for He113 fighters and give them a wide berth. Again, the German ruse worked. RAF combat reports from this period are filled with references to the dreaded He113.

On the British side the burst of German successes brought to a head disputes that had been simmering for some time. These disagreements were between the commanders of 11 Group and 12 Group – and it was Dowding who had to find a solution.

As RAF fighter tactics had developed in the war so far, there was a clear pattern that was to be followed if at all possible when tackling incoming German raids. Once radar had picked up a raid, the controller would scramble two squadrons to intercept. If at all possible these should be one Spitfire and one Hurricane squadron. The Spitfire squadron would attack first, flying in at a high altitude to tackle the fighter escort. The Hurricanes would follow seconds later to attack the now, hopefully, unprotected bombers. Whenever possible the interception was to take place over the sea, but it was accepted that most interceptions would take place over land – especially in the Dover area where the strip of sea was narrow.

However, the improved German tactics meant that the radar operators had trouble sorting out the real raids from the decoys. Fighters were often not scrambled until it was too late for a Spitfire and Hurricane squadron to be brought together to cooperate. Sometimes two units of Hurricanes were sent in, or two of Spitfires. More often the supposedly closely coordinated attacks occurred in piecemeal fashion, and sometimes a single squadron would be faced with tackling more than 100 German aircraft alone.

It was in these circumstances that Air Vice Marshal Keith Park, the head of 11 Group, was authorised to request help from his neighbouring Groups. Air Vice Marshal Sir A. Quintin Brand, commander of 10 Group, was not in a position to offer much help. He had only 10 squadrons, one of them equipped with biplane Gladiators, and most of them were deployed to protect Plymouth, Exeter and Bristol. His controllers were, however, instructed to send squadrons to help 11 Group whenever asked to do so, which provided some relief to the western areas of 11 Group's responsibilities.

In a much better position to help was 12 Group, commanded by Air Vice Marshal Trafford Leigh-Mallory. This Group had 14 squadrons, most of which were located in East Anglia or north of London as the pre-war RAF had expected German bombers to come

The New Zealander Air Vice Marshal Keith Park commanded 11 Group of Fighter Command, and with it all the Surrey air bases, during the Battle of Britain. He left 11 Group after the battle, moving to take command of the air defence of Malta as that island came under heavy pounding from the Italian air force. He retired from the RAF in 1946 with the rank of Marshal and returned to his native islands where he took up a series of civic posts. He died in 1975.

Air Vice Marshal Trafford Leigh-Mallory commanded 12 Group of Fighter Command in the Battle of Britain. In the autumn of 1940 he was appointed to command 11 Group, which included all the bases in Surrey. He was promoted to lead Fighter Command in 1942. He was killed in an air crash in 1944.

in off the North Sea. These squadrons could take off and be over 11 Group air space within minutes.

However, Leigh-Mallory had his own ideas about fighter tactics and was keen to put them into practice. His tactic was to become known as the 'Big Wing'. Put simply he envisaged the answer to the large German fighter escorts to be attacks conducted by formations of RAF fighters at least three squadrons strong and preferably four or five. Leigh-Mallory began forming his fighters up into a Big Wing before dispatching them south to aid 11 Group. When they made contact with German formations, the 12 Group fighters invariably inflicted heavy casualties for light losses suffered by themselves. Leigh-Mallory felt vindicated.

Park, however, was furious. The time taken for the Big Wing to form up meant that it arrived much later than the fighters would have done if they had been dispatched south from their bases as individual squadrons. That meant that the German bombers had usually bombed their targets – often Park's fighter bases – and were on their way home before the Big Wing arrived. More than once the Germans had escaped entirely unscathed. Furthermore, Park questioned the good results gained by the Big Wing, pointing out that because they arrived late the Bf109 escorts had usually already departed for France due to their smaller fuel tanks.

The arguments reached boiling point when Biggin Hill, an 11 Group base, was hit by six raids in just three days. After the final raid, the official report read, in part, 'Practically no buildings left to damage, all main services and communications destroyed.' The Big Wing arrived just in time to see the smoke columns rising up into the sky but too late to tackle the raiders.

Dowding had his hands full organising not just the fighters, but also the barrage balloons, anti-aircraft guns, searchlights and other ground defences. The last thing he needed was a dispute between two senior commanders. He sent for Park and Leigh-Mallory and told them that the situation was too grave for petty disputes to get in the way of fighting the Germans. They had to get on and that was that. Then he sent them packing. The dressing down alleviated the dispute, but did nothing to temper the ill-feeling which was to surface again once the pressure of combat eased.

Although the senior commanders did their best, the dispute could not be hidden from the officers lower down the command chain. Rivalry between squadrons could be intense at times, and that transferred over to Group as well. By mid-September most pilots were aware of the Big Wing controversy, though they were unaware of the detail. In late September there was to occur an incident that brought matters to a head.

No.253 Squadron took off from Kenley to patrol over Canterbury at 15,000 ft to meet an incoming German raid. The commander, Flt. Lt. Myles Duke-Woolley, decided on his own initiative to climb up to 28,000 ft as some recent German raids had come in at a greater height than the radar had estimated. A few minutes later the Big Wing approached from the north at 20,000 ft. They were heading due south to intercept a different German raid crossing the coast near Folkestone. Since the Canterbury raid had not materialised, Duke-Woolley decided to follow the Big Wing to see what they were after. As the Hurricanes swung in behind and above the Big Wing, the 12 Group pilots spotted them for the first time. Thinking that the Hurricanes were Bf109s, the Big Wing began to circle so that the 'enemy' could not get behind them. Puzzled, Duke-Woolley also began to circle on the assumption that the Big Wing commander was waiting for a German formation to arrive. After several minutes of this, the Big Wing began to run low on fuel, so it turned off north to return to base while No.253 Squadron, by now equally low on fuel, returned to Kenley.

The recriminations that followed saw Leigh-Mallory condemning the freelance movements of Park's squadron, while Park denounced the Big Wing's shortage of fuel caused by the time it took to form up before heading south. The men of No.253 naturally mocked the pilots of 12 Group for their inability to tell the difference between a Hurricane and a Bf109.

At the start of September 1940, however, these disputes were only just beginning to filter down to squadron level. Most pilots were naturally more concerned with staying alive and shooting down Germans than the ongoing spats between senior officers.

At Kenley the month began badly. The morning of 1 September had seen two scrambles, but no actual combat. Then, at 1.50 pm a third scramble was sounded and No.85 Squadron roared off to meet a force of 200 German aircraft that was crossing the coast near Hastings. Undetected by radar or the Observer Corps, however, a squadron of Bf109s had peeled off at great height and raced inland to watch for fighters taking off to intercept the raid. The German pilots spotted the Hurricanes of No.85 Squadron lifting off from Kenley, got behind them and then screamed down to launch a surprise and devastating bounce attack.

First to be hit was the lead Hurricane, flown by Flying Officer Patrick Woods-Scawen. Woods-Scawen was one of the leading pilots of the squadron. During May and June he had fought several actions over France, shooting down six German aircraft. In an action over Dunkirk he had got separated from his squadron, then spotted eight German fighters beneath him. Getting into a high speed dive he had gone down with guns blazing in a single, swooping pass that left two Germans crashing earthwards to destruction. He was awarded a DFC after Dunkirk with his citation reading 'He has displayed great courage, endurance and leadership.'

But on 1 September his luck ran out. It is likely that, as he was the first to be shot down, he did not even see the Messerschmitt that killed him. His Hurricane went into a savage spin and crashed heavily into a meadow, instantly bursting into flames. The pilot's body was found five days later in deep undergrowth a few hundred yards away. The parachute had not opened and it was unclear if it had failed or if Woods-Scawen had been thrown clear from his plane after he was already dead.

Next to be hit was the Hurricane flown by Sergeant Glendon Booth. The first he knew of the attack was when a hail of cannon shells smashed into his engine in front of his cockpit. Then the cockpit itself shattered into fragments as gunfire lanced through it. Realising his aircraft was doomed, Booth clambered out of his cockpit and jumped. Unknown to him, however, a cannon shell splinter had ripped through his parachute pack. As soon as the parachute opened, it went into a vicious spin and became quite uncontrollable. Helpless to alter the course of his descent, Booth slammed into a telegraph pole. The impact broke an arm and a leg, and caused horrific internal injuries. Booth was taken off to hospital where he seemed to be recovering when his kidneys failed and he died.

Third to be hit was the Hurricane of Flying Officer Arthur Gowers. He had been with No.85 Squadron since 1938 and was one of the very few pre-war pilots still to be flying with the unit. He had three confirmed German aircraft to his credit, but that did nothing to save him on 1 September. His fighter burst into flames, so Gowers baled out to land safely near Chelsham. He had suffered minor burns and was taken to hospital, never to return to No.85. He was killed in 1943 when leading No.183 Squadron's Typhoons on a raid to Cherbourg.

The fourth Hurricane to be hit in the high-speed clash that day was flown by Pilot Officer A. Lewis. The aircraft was peppered with bullets,

A Hurricane MkII. This variant was armed with two 40 mm cannon mounted in under-wing pods and entered service in early 1942. It was used mainly as a low-level ground attack weapon and proved to be devastatingly effective against panzers and other vehicles.

A Messerschmitt Bf109 shot down over Surrey in September 1940.

but did not catch fire. Lewis managed to nurse it back to Kenley. Sergeant John Ellis did not return to Kenley that day and by nightfall had been posted as missing. It was not until 1992 that a chance discovery of some wreckage led to the excavation of an overgrown field near Chelsfield in Kent. The mangled remains of Ellis's Hurricane were found there. His body was given a decent burial.

Minutes after this catastrophic battle, a group of the German bombers arrived to pound Kenley airbase. The bombing was scattered and poorly aimed. The airfield was peppered with craters but no important buildings were hit and nobody was killed. Several nearby houses were destroyed.

On 4 September the Germans came to Surrey again. The morning began with a series of decoy raids made by small groups of fast-flying fighters on apparently random courses over southern England. Fighters were scrambled to meet them, but the Germans did not hesitate or turn to fight and were invariably gone by the time the RAF aircraft got into position.

The German fighters did, however, claim a victim in the form of the Canadian Pilot Officer Gray Trueman of No.253 Squadron. He was scrambled from Kenley but when the flight levelled off he was no longer with it. In fact his aircraft had plunged to earth soon after take off. It had come down in Tudor Close, Banstead, in an almost vertical

Sergeant John Ellis of No.85 Squadron took off from Kenley on 1 September 1940, but did not return. His fate was a complete mystery until 1992 when the wreck of his fighter was discovered buried in a field some miles to the east. His aircraft must have struck the ground at great speed to bury itself out of view in this way.

dive with its engine at full power. It was presumed that Trueman had blacked out for some reason, but nobody ever found out what had really caused the crash.

Soon after noon a fresh force of German aircraft was detected by radar over northern France, near Calais. The force divided, the smaller part heading to Gravesend, the rest pushing west along the Channel. A second force peeled off to attack Eastbourne. Then a third force struck off for Tunbridge Wells and a fourth went for Worthing. A fifth group headed north-west across Sussex and Surrey at high speed. They proved to be a formation of Bf110 aircraft, each one loaded with a ton of bombs. This time the raid was picked up by radar and accurately tracked by the Observer Corps. At first the target was unclear as the Germans' route was taking them close to both Kenley and Croydon. The Germans droned on, ignoring both. Then they turned to port and headed for Brooklands.

The surprise was total, the fast-moving Bf110s arriving before an air raid siren could be sounded. The target was the Vickers factory that was manufacturing Wellington bombers for the RAF. Tragically the army gun crew that was supposed to be manning a Bofors anti-aircraft gun were having their lunch along with the bulk of the work force in the canteen when the bombs began to fall. Everyone bolted for the air raid shelters that dotted the grounds of the factory. Not all of them made it.

In all 83 workers were killed outright during the raid and another 176 were injured seriously enough to need to spend one or more days in hospital. Another 243 were injured, but did not require hospitalisation. The Vickers factory was devastated and around two months' worth of production was lost. Bravely, however, over 85 per cent of the surviving work force reported for duty the next day and were put to work helping to clear away the rubble.

Meanwhile, No.253 Squadron was racing in from Croydon to the rescue. They arrived too late to spoil the Germans' aim, but pounced as the Bf110s swung away to the south. Flight Lieutenant Cambridge targeted a Bf110 as he came diving down from the left of the fleeing machine. A long burst from the Hurricane's guns caused the port engine of the Messerschmitt to burst into flames and the aircraft went down. One crew member baled out, but the other was killed. A second raider fell to the guns of Flight Lieutenant Wedgewood. This time there were no survivors as the German aircraft ploughed into a wood near Horsley. Four other German aircraft were damaged, but got away.

Three RAF cooks prepare to serve a meal to ground-crew working in the open at a base 'somewhere in southern England'. Although not usually thought of as combat staff, even cooks risked death if their air base came under attack from the Luftwaffe.

Wellington bomber production at Vickers, Brooklands. The basket weave construction was designed by Barnes Wallis.

Goering judged the fast-moving raids by Bf110 bombers to have caused great damage through accurate bombing and though the cost to the Germans had been heavy it had not been inordinately so. On 6 September the Bf110 bombers were back. Once again Brooklands was one of the targets. Again the Germans launched numerous dummy raids to confuse the defenders but this time the raiders were intercepted just as they were starting their bombing run. None was shot down, but their aim was spoiled and no great damage was done.

One of the Messerschmitts was bounced by a Hurricane pilot limping home to Biggin Hill with a misfiring engine. The German crashed near Crowhurst. One crew member got out alive and was arrested by a squad of Canadian soldiers billeted nearby. The other German seemed to be unconscious and was still strapped in when the Bf110 exploded. Nobody ever came to retrieve his badly burned body, so the Canadians buried him close to the wreckage of his aircraft. So far as is known his body is still there.

Sergeant Leslie Tweed of No.111 Squadron had a lucky escape that day.

He got into combat with a group of high-flying bombers at around 25,000 ft over Woldingham. A stream of bullets from a bomber shattered his canopy and concussed him into unconsciousness. When he came to his Hurricane was down to 1,000 ft and falling rapidly. He hurriedly jumped clear and pulled his ripcord, only to black out again. He landed heavily, but survived.

That evening No.111 Squadron received another piece of good news to add to the fortuitous escape of Sergeant Tweed. The popular Flight Lieutenant Stanley Connors was awarded a bar to the DFC that he had won during the fighting over France. The earlier medal had been awarded for a remarkable two days of combat flying when, despite being heavily outnumbered on each of four missions he had shot down three Heinkel He111 bombers, two Junkers Ju88 bombers and a single Bf109 fighter. The bar was awarded for his actions in the last week of August when he downed another four enemy aircraft, bringing his total to a round dozen. Sadly, Connors did not live to receive his medal as he was shot down and killed soon after the award.

More happily, Sergeant William Dymond of the same squadron did survive to collect the DFM that he was awarded the same day. When writing to commend him for the DFM his squadron commander had commented, 'This grand fighting pilot has shown a great offensive spirit. He has shot down eight enemy aircraft and has shown himself to be a leader of great promise. I strongly recommend him for the award of the Distinguished Flying Medal.'

That day's fighting would prove to be a crucial turning point, though nobody in Fighter Command was yet aware of it. The Germans were about to change their plans drastically.

Dornier Do17Z

Type:	Five crew medium bomber
Engine:	2 x 1000 hp Bramo Fafnir 323P
Wingspan:	59 ft
Length:	51 ft 9 in
Height:	14 ft 11 in
Weight:	Empty 13,145 lb Loaded 18,937 lb
Armament:	6 x 7.9 mm machine guns in various positions
Bombload:	2205 lb
Max speed:	263 mph
Ceiling:	26,740 ft
Range:	720 miles
Production:	1,200

Dornier's Do17 range of bombers began in 1934 when Lufthansa rejected a Dornier design for a fast mail plane. By late 1935 Dornier had converted the prototype to be a bomber with an internal bomb bay, machine-gun mountings and a glazed nose. This entered Luftwaffe service in 1938 as the Do17M, a bomber, and the Do17P, a long-range reconnaissance scout. It quickly acquired the nickname of 'Flying Pencil' due to its thin fuselage. Experience in the Spanish Civil War highlighted problems with the bomber version, which by 1938 was replaced by the Do17Z, to which the figures given here apply. This had a much enlarged front section of fuselage to house extra guns and other equipment. An export version was produced for Germany's allies, such as Hungary, but by 1942 the Luftwaffe was phasing the Do17 out of front line service. The Do17Z equipped nine Gruppen in four Kampfgeschwaders when the first attacks on Channel convoys were carried out in July 1940. Soon after operations over mainland Great Britain commenced, the bomber's deficiencies were exposed. More machine guns were added and the new tactics were employed, but losses continued at such a rate that by October 1940 the type's role as a front-line day bomber was effectively over.

Chapter 6

Defending London

The morning of **7 September 1940** dawned bright and clear. At Kenley, Croydon and other fighter stations across southern England the pilots trooped down to dispersal ready to scramble or went up to fly routine patrols. Everyone expected a fresh German onslaught to begin soon after dawn. Nothing came. Across RAF Fighter Command men and women fidgeted and paced restlessly.

At RAF Kenley there had been a change. The Operations Room that had previously been in a virtually unprotected brick building on the base had now been moved over a mile away to the main shopping street of Caterham. No.11 Godstone Road had been, until shortly before that, a butcher's and abbatoir, but it was now standing empty due to the wartime shortage of meat.

Then RAF personnel moved in to whitewash the windows, block the front door and reconfigure the interior, while telephone engineers laid in hundreds of lines. The rooms facing the street were made into rest rooms and cafés so that no sound from the vital work taking place in the old abbatoir could be heard from the street. It was here that the operations room was to be located for the rest of the Battle of Britain and through the Blitz. The only real problem was that there was only one toilet – and that was on the top floor.

Secrecy was everything. The British secret services were uncertain of

A scene from a sector control room. WAAFs move the markers indicating aircraft on the map in the foreground while behind them more senior staff handle incoming messages.

how many German spies were operating in Britain – as it turned out, very few – so steps were taken not to draw attention to the converted shop. Staff to man the centre were transported down to the rear of the shop in an unmarked civilian-looking bus, then whisked back to RAF Kenley by the same means at the end of their shift. No service personnel were allowed to leave the premises to wander around the town. Lord Beaverbrook, then Minister for Munitions, came down to see how it was all working in such a confined and hastily-converted space.

But on this sunny September morning the staff at Kenley Operations Room had little to do. A few decoy raids came up over France, circled for a time and then landed, but no German formations headed over the Channel towards England. It was a deceptive calm.

At around 4 pm a force of 150 German aircraft headed north from France, crossed the British coast at Dungeness and continued north. Then the radar operators gasped and double-checked their equipment. Stacked up behind this first raid was a force of Luftwaffe aircraft larger than anything anyone had ever seen before, so large that it swamped the radar sets and made counting the aircraft impossible. In fact, there were over 1000 aircraft in the formation – two thirds of them fighters.

The horde came thundering north, crossed the Kent coast and droned on. Dowding plotted their course and calculated that they were heading for his airfields in Kent – Biggin Hill, Manston and the like, that had suffered so badly already. The squadrons from Kenley and Croydon were scrambled to patrol over Maidstone and Folkestone to catch the raiders as they split up to bomb the airfields. The Hurricanes circled alone but no German bombers came into sight.

Against all expectations the Germans neither split up nor diverted towards the airfields of Fighter Command. Instead they continued on north to the Thames estuary, then wheeled left and headed for central London. Dowding had been caught out. His fighters were in the wrong place, and would need to land to refuel before they could get to London. For once 11 Group and 12 Group cooperated well. A squadron of Polish pilots from north of the Thames, No.303 Squadron, attacked the Germans over London. To the amazement of their British commander, Squadron Leader A.S. Forbes, the Poles closed to less than 100 yards before opening fire. Other fighter squadrons arrived to attack, but they found themselves confronted by another new tactic used by the Luftwaffe. The close fighter escort was now positioned on either side of the bombers, as well as just above it. And the high-level escort was in front of the bombers, with an even higher escort at over 30,000 ft positioned behind. Those squadrons that did reach the German formation made little impression. The few German bombers shot down that day were mostly claimed by anti-aircraft guns.

The squadrons flying out of Surrey were having an even more frustrating day. They landed from their fruitless mission, refuelled and took off again – only to be sent to the wrong place again so that they missed the German bombers on their way back to France. Meanwhile, the Bf109 fighters had raced back to France, refuelled and were now roaming the skies of southern England looking for victims.

Pilot Officer C. Bodie, out of Kenley, ran into them over Folkestone and his engine was quickly reduced to scrap by cannon shells. Bodie was uninjured, and his Spitfire appeared to be relatively unscathed so he opted to glide down for an unpowered landing. Unable to find a field large enough in time, Bodie had to land with his wheels up. This reduced the

Bombed out civilians gather their surviving possessions in the street before abandoning their ruined house. Such refugees might go to stay with relatives, or the government might billet them on more or less willing neighbours.

Londoners peer into the ruins of their house in the East End. The growing concentration of bombing on London was designed to smash civilian morale and force Britain to accept a negotiated peace.

distance needed for the aircraft to stop but wrecked the fighter and made for a very bumpy end to the flight.

Another pilot to encounter the roving Messerschmitts was the South African Squadron Leader Caesar Hull. Hull had led his No.43 Squadron out of Tangmere in Sussex after refuelling to try to reach the German bombers. He somehow got separated from the rest of the formation and was alone when he was pounced on by four Bf109 fighters over Coulsdon. Unlike Bodie, he did not survive.

That night the bombers returned to London in darkness. They did not need accurate night navigation equipment as vast areas of the docks and East End were aflame. The bombers poured their loads into the conflagration below, adding to the destruction and the mayhem.

The dramatic change of plan by the Luftwaffe, to target London instead of the Fighter Command bases, had come about due to Hitler's intervention. Hitler had already been forced to postpone the date for the invasion of Britain from the first week of September to the 15th. The state of the tides and other factors meant that if the invasion were not made on that day, it would not be possible until early October – and by that date there would be no guarantee of the relatively calm seas needed for the river and canal barges that were to carry the supplies of the invasion force to cross the Channel. When the decision had been made to postpone the invasion, Hitler had ordered his staff to look for other ways to bring Britain to a negotiated peace.

The German navy went off to draw up plans for a sustained U-boat campaign against convoys of merchant ships heading for Britain. The army half-heartedly suggested invading Ireland as a soft option. The Luftwaffe, however, suggested pounding Britain's cities to rubble. This option had worked in Poland and Holland, and the mere threat of it had persuaded the French to abandon Paris to the Germans as an 'open city', allowing it to be captured instead of destroyed. Several of Goering's senior commanders had never been keen on the invasion idea, believing that it would lead to massive casualties among their crews, and had long favoured city bombing. They pointed out that attacks on British ports and transport centres would complement the naval strategy of the slow starvation of Britain. Britain would surrender in the spring of 1941, they confidently predicted, or if not then by the following autumn at the latest.

But Goering knew something that his senior officers did not. Hitler was already planning to attack Russia in May or June of 1941. This massive land offensive not only meant that Luftwaffe forces would need to be removed from the British offensive from February 1941 onwards to prepare, but it also meant that the Reich's manufacturing capacity would be poured into tanks, artillery and infantry equipment. The numbers of bombers needed to pound Britain to destruction or U-boats needed to starve her would simply not be available.

If Britain were to be bombed to the peace table, the offensive had to be quick and devastating. It was for this reason that Goering chose to target London on 7 September, rather than the assorted naval bases and merchant marine ports that the German navy and most of his own staff wanted. Goering hoped that by destroying Britain's capital city he would both destroy the government infrastructure and also deal such a terrible blow to morale that Britain would choose peace. And Hitler had made it clear that he would offer Britain generous terms to get her out of the war before the invasion of Russia began.

In the short term, Goering's emphasis on London paid off but it would later work against him. The concentration on London meant that whenever Dowding saw a large raid heading over the Channel he could be fairly certain that it was heading for London and deploy his fighters accordingly. If the Luftwaffe had been bombing a variety of ports and transport centres, Dowding would have been kept guessing and so might have made mistakes similar to that on 7 September.

The weather on 8 September was poor, but the next raid of the new phase came on 9 September. This time the Germans came over in a series of formations, with numerous decoy raids and feints to confuse the defenders. The Surrey squadrons were scrambled to intercept raiders coming north over Kent, while squadrons from 12 Group were ordered to come south to defend the skies over Surrey.

No.605 Squadron was by this date at Croydon, led by Squadron Leader Walter Churchill DFC DSO, and it was sent out towards Maidstone. They found themselves faced by 90 Heinkel He111 bombers, with an escort of an estimated 60 Bf109 fighters. Undeterred the 12 Hurricanes went into the attack. Flying behind Churchill was Flight Lieutenant Archibald McKellar, who was about to have a most interesting afternoon.

As McKellar attacked he selected a Heinkel as his target, held his fire until he was about 300 yards away and then pushed the trigger button on his control stick. His eight machine guns spat out bullets, but he was unprepared for what followed. The Heinkel in front of him suddenly

Walter Churchill of No.3 Squadron left Surrey for France when war was declared to form part of the Advanced Air Strike Force (AASF) that was to operate from sub-standard French airfields through the winter of 1939-40 and through to the blitzkrieg of May 1940. He later served with No.605 Squadron at Croydon.

disappeared in a vast ball of orange flame – his bullets had set off the full seven ton bomb load. Dragging desperately at his controls to veer away from the deadly blast, McKellar watched in amazement as flying debris from the exploding bomber lanced through the formation. Two more bombers went down, knocked from the sky by the blast and the flying wreckage.

Not wanting to hang about to face the Bf109 escort, the pilots of No.605 headed back toward Croydon. On his way west McKellar came across a lone Bf109 apparently on the prowl. He shot it down, bringing his score for the sortie up to four. A week later he learned that he had been awarded the DFC. He was given a bar to the medal only four weeks later, by which time he had successfully shot down another eight German aircraft. Five of those aircraft had been shot down in a single day – four Bf109s in a single dogfight in the morning and a fifth fighter that afternoon.

McKellar was to be killed in October in a moment of carelessness witnessed by his squadron comrade Duke-Woolley. The squadron was over Dover and near the limit of its fuel when a formation of Bf109 fighters was spotted heading out to sea. No.605 went down to attack, McKellar shooting down one Bf109. He then seemed to relax, thinking the action over. In fact the Bf109s had turned to follow the departing Hurricanes. One got on McKellar's tail and shot him down. When he was killed, McKellar had a score of 21 German aircraft confirmed destroyed, three probably destroyed and three damaged.

Another high-scoring pilot with No.605 Squadron was Flight Lieutenant Christopher Currant who shot down seven German aircraft in September, a feat that saw him awarded the DFC. In October he shot down six more, and got a bar to his medal.

The fighters from 12 Group had not fared so well over Surrey. A small raid had been spotted heading for Farnborough and they went into the attack. Five Hurricanes were lost for only three Germans shot down. One of those Germans, a Bf110 that came down in Worcester Park, provoked a mystery. The Bf110 had a crew of two, but the wreckage of this particular machine contained three men inside. The remains of the mysterious third man were so badly damaged that all that could be discerned was that he was a medical orderly. What he was doing on the fighter remains unknown. Post-war study of Luftwaffe records did not help as they recorded that the crew of the aircraft on the fatal mission had been only Otto Kramp and Albrecht Pfaffelhuber. The three bodies were buried in one grave in Surbiton cemetery.

On 11 September the pattern was repeated with squadrons from outside Surrey fighting over the county and suffering for it. Two Spitfires and a Hurricane were shot down, but only one German, a Heinkel He111, was brought down.

On 13 September No.501 Squadron were scrambled to intercept a formation of bombers heading for central London. The Hurricanes did not get there in time, so the combat that followed took place over central London itself in full view of those Londoners who had not dived for the air raid shelters.

Among the pilots of No.501 Squadron that day was a young Sergeant James Lacey. He had already been awarded a DFM for his fighting over France in May and June as the panzers had swept forwards. He had downed five enemy aircraft during that period and the French military found time to honour him with the Croix de Guerre before they surrendered to the Germans. Neither Lacey nor his comrades rated his skill as a pilot particularly highly and when it came to aerobatics he was left standing by others. He was, however, a crack shot both on the ground and in the air and it was to this that he later ascribed his phenomenal success during combat flying.

On 13 September he joined his squadron in attacking the formation of Heinkels over London, then spotted one bomber low down attacking Buckingham Palace, no less. Lacey dived down and with his first burst of gunfire killed the rear gunner. The Heinkel then vanished into cloud, and Lacey followed it in. Re-emerging into bright sunlight, Lacey found himself directly behind the bomber and again opened fire. By this time a different crew member was manning the rear gun and shot back. Lacey's engine radiator was smashed, the engine overheated and caught fire – but nothing put Lacey off sending a second and devastating burst of shots that set the bomber on fire in turn. Baling out, Lacey saw parachutes drop from the German bomber, which then nose-dived into the ground.

Two weeks later Lacey received news that he had been awarded a bar to his DFM. By this time his score of German aircraft destroyed stood at 19 confirmed, with another 6 unconfirmed and a dozen or more damaged. He was to finish the year with no fewer than 23 confirmed kills, and was commissioned to be a Pilot Officer shortly afterwards. Lacey then left No.501 Squadron around the time that the unit left Kenley. After a period as an instructor he joined No.602 Squadron, a Spitfire unit, but then his famous shooting abilities saw him recruited to test new weapons – in particular the under-wing rockets that would later prove to be such devastating ground-attack weapons for Fighter Command. In 1943 he went to India to train pilots in dogfighting and in 1945 he returned to combat in Spitfires over Burma. It was there that he shot down his 28th and final enemy aircraft – a Nakajima Ki43 Hayabusa single-engined fighter that was known to the Allies as the 'Oscar'.

One of the effects of the growing Luftwaffe emphasis on London was that the fighter bases and fighter squadrons had time to recover from the constant pounding that they had been receiving. Aircraft could now be properly repaired, men rested and facilities restored. This was just as well for on 15 September the Luftwaffe made their greatest effort to date.

The day again dawned bright and sunny, but this time the Luftwaffe were up early with decoys and feints. Then, around 10.40 am, the radar picked up what was clearly a major formation gathering over Calais. At 11.15 am No.253 and No.501 Squadrons were scrambled from Kenley and ordered to attack a formation of German aircraft coming in over the Kent coast.

The commander of No.253 Squadron, Squadron Leader Gerry Edge (who had been awarded a DFC only two days earlier), had developed the theory that attacking bombers head on was the best form of assault. The closing speed was nerve-racking, but the tactic did make the German formation break up so that the individual bombers were easier targets. On this occasion he decided to put his plan into effect using the entire squadron.

As they raced toward the Germans, the pilots of No.253 saw that the enemy formation was composed of 28 Dornier Do17 bombers with an escort of over 100 fighters. Hoping for the best, the Hurricane fighters roared in with guns blazing. As predicted the bombers began to weave and peel off as they were attacked. In all 17 bombers were hit and fell out of the formation. How many were actually shot down is unclear as the Hurricane pilots were speeding away with throttles wide open to escape the 100 fighters that were coming down fast. When No.501 Squadron arrived, the remaining German bombers jettisoned their bombs and turned for home.

That afternoon a massed formation of 200 Dornier and Heinkel bombers escorted by 500 fighters came north over Kent to attack London. The Surrey squadrons were among those sent off to attack them. The Hurricanes from Surrey did their best to get through to attack the bombers, but were fought to a standstill by the escorting fighters, on this day under the command of the veteran Adolf Galland. It was with mixed feelings that the Surrey pilots learned that after they had left the fray, Galland and his fighters had turned for France, their fuel exhausted by the dogfighting. It was at this point that the Big Wing from 12 Group arrived to find the bombers without an escort and inflicted heavy casualties.

Shot down in the dogfighting was Pilot Officer Graves of No.253 Squadron. Graves was a cousin of the novelist Robert Graves. This was a time when rumours were circulating that German pilots were machine-gunning RAF pilots as they dangled from their parachutes. The pilots of No.253 had decided that the best way to escape such a fate was to drop well clear of the fighting before pulling on the ripcord to open the parachute.

Finding himself baling out at 17,000 ft in the midst of a dogfight with Germans all around, Graves decided to drop well clear before opening his parachute. He fell into cloud at around 7,000 ft and came hurtling out the bottom of the cloud rather closer to the ground than he had expected. He yanked on his ripcord, the parachute opened and his headlong fall to the ground was snapped savagely to an end just 150 ft from the ground. It had been a close thing.

The next day, 16 September, the Luftwaffe did not come despite perfect flying weather. They never again came in such numbers and with such determination. On 17 September, Hitler accepted that the RAF Fighter Command had not been destroyed – something that had long been

An unidentified team of RAF ground-crew at RAF Kenley sometime in 1940 or 1941. These men worked long hours under great pressure to ensure that the fighters continued to fly.

accepted as a pre-condition for any invasion of Britain. With the poor autumn weather now closing in, the invasion of Britain, codenamed Operation Sealion, was postponed until the spring of 1941.

Hitler would return to the problem of how to defeat Britain at a military conference held in January 1941. By that date he was committed to an invasion of Russia later that year and could not afford to spare the resources for an invasion of Britain. It was decided instead that Britain should be ground down to a position of destitution by food shortages and financial bankruptcy. This would be achieved by the Italians, who had joined the war in June 1940, capturing Malta and the Suez Canal in the Mediterranean while Franco, the fascist dictator of Spain, would be persuaded to occupy Gibraltar. The German U-boats would attack convoys in the Atlantic to reduce food supplies to Britain. The Luftwaffe would remain committed to an aerial assault on London and other British

The Battle of Britain Monument on the Embankment in London,
just outside the Ministry of Defence.

*London's docklands burns in the autumn of 1940 as the Luftwaffe's
night-bombing campaign reaches its peak.*

cities until April 1941, when they would be withdrawn to join the invasion
of Russia.

As far as the Luftwaffe was concerned, the conference merely confirmed what they had been doing since the massed raids of 15 September. Daylight raids were being conducted by small formations of fast-flying Bf110 aircraft carrying bombs and by the almost-as-speedy Junkers Ju88, which could carry twice as heavy a bomb load. These raids were carried out at speed, and often at high altitude in the hope that the raiders could be in and out again before RAF fighters could intercept them. Bf109 fighters continued to escort the bombers, but they also launched wide-ranging sweeps of their own, shooting up ground targets and hoping to pounce on RAF fighters if they could be caught at a disadvantage.

The longer nights of autumn and winter gave much greater scope to the nocturnal bombing of city areas than had the summer. Bombing at night was much safer for the bombers as they could not be seen so easily by either fighter pilots or anti-aircraft gunners. They were, equally, unable to see much of their targets. If individual factories were being targeted this would make bombing hopelessly inaccurate, but when the objective was simply to target city centres then even the most inaccurate bombing was effective enough. With these night raids, the Luftwaffe hoped both to break civilian morale and to disrupt communications and transport links. Both, it was hoped, would exert pressure on the British government and help persuade them to make peace come the spring of 1941.

Messerschmitt Bf110

Type: Two seat long-range fighter
Engine: 2 x 1100 hp Daimler-Benz DB601A
Wingspan: 53 ft 4 in
Length: 39 ft 8 in
Height: 11 ft 6 in
Weight: Empty 9920 lb
Loaded 15,300 lb
Armament: 2 x 20 mm cannon and 4 x 7.9 mm machine guns in nose plus 1 x 7.9 mm machine gun in rear cockpit
Max speed: 349 mph
Ceiling: 32,000 ft
Range: 565 miles
Production: 6,050

Before the war began the Luftwaffe, unlike some other air forces, had worried that their bombers might not be able to fend off attacks by fighters. The need for an escort fighter with a similar range to the bombers was recognised, but the additional fuel tanks would make the resulting aircraft heavy. The answer, the Germans thought, was to provide twin engines and a heavy armament to give increased speed and hitting power to make up for a lack of nimbleness. The Bf110 entered service in July 1938 and by the time of the Battle of Britain was available in no fewer than seven variants, mostly concerned with armament or increased range. The figures given above are for the C5 model. After its lack of success against the Spitfire and Hurricane, the 110 was redesigned to be either a fast bomber or a night-fighter in a further 20 variants. It remained in production to the end of 1944.

Chapter 7

The Blitz

One of the first signs Surrey had of the change of tactics came on 20 September when a Junkers Ju88 fell out of the sky for no known reason to crash into houses in Merton. The sole survivor of the crew, the bomb aimer, had baled out as he felt the aircraft begin its fatal dive and could not explain what had happened. However, it was clear that the bomber had been heading for central London by night.

At 8 am the following day another Junkers Ju88 bombed the Vickers factory at Brooklands that had suffered so badly from a raid some weeks earlier. Two bombs went off causing some damage, but the third went through the factory roof then bounced through a wall and came to rest just outside. Lieutenant J. Patton, a Canadian engineer, arrived from the bomb disposal squad. He recruited factory workers to help him hitch the bomb to a truck, and then towed it for 200 yards to a location where it was later set off, exploding harmlessly.

One of the busiest days of air fighting over Surrey was 27 September. The day's activity began when a force of Bf110 heavy fighters roared overhead at altitude, but it was only a decoy raid designed to lure up the British fighters so that they would be on the ground refuelling when the real raid went in. The ruse did not work particularly well, partly because the following raid by Junkers Ju88 bombers lacked the planned escort of Bf109 fighters due to an error over timing by the German fighters. As a result, the Junkers bombers arrived with only a close escort of Bf110s.

Nevertheless the first aircraft to go down was a Hurricane of No.501 Squadron operating out of Kenley. Sergeant Victor Ekins was fighting a Bf110 when a second German fighter attacked and set his aircraft on fire. Ekins suffered minor burns before he managed to bale out. His Hurricane crashed near Godstone at 9.15 am, but strong winds meant that he floated down near Sevenoaks in Kent. He did not return to combat flying until November 1942 but managed to survive the war.

Five minutes later a Spitfire of No.92 Squadron from Biggin Hill was plunging from the sky to crash near Walton-on-Thames railway station. The pilot, Flight Sergeant Charles Sydney, was killed instantly. Next to fall was a Junkers Ju88 which crashed at 9.30 am at South Holmwood. Over the next 20 minutes four more aircraft came down, two Hurricanes and two Bf110 fighters – one of which crashed on Gatwick airfield and only narrowly missed the hangars and old pre-war terminal buildings.

On the whole, Dowding preferred not to publicise the deeds of individual pilots, and certainly did his best to stop them becoming media celebrities as was common in Germany. He felt that to do this not only put too much pressure on the pilot in question, but was also unfair on the others who faced equal danger and peril in the course of their combat duties. Nevertheless, some pilots did get their names plastered over the national news. One such was Pilot Officer Kenneth MacKenzie of No.501 Squadron when flying out of Kenley in late September.

MacKenzie had been on patrol near Hythe with Squadron Leader Hogan when they spotted a lone Bf109. The two Hurricane pilots fought a swift and successful battle that ended with the German fighter diving into the sea. Hogan, out of ammunition, returned to Kenley at this point, but MacKenzie decided to continue with the patrol route alone.

As he flew on, MacKenzie spotted a formation of eight Bf109s coming towards him at 23,000 ft. Realising that he had not been spotted, MacKenzie manoeuvred to launch an attack on the rearmost fighter. He poured in a burst of fire, and saw a stream of glycol emerge from the German's engine. The Messerschmitt rolled over and went into a dive. Wanting to make sure of his kill, MacKenzie followed the German down. The dive turned out to be a ruse, and the German levelled out above the sea and headed for home once more. MacKenzie attacked again, sending a long burst toward the German which stopped only when he ran out of ammunition. To MacKenzie's surprise and intense annoyance the burst of fire had no obvious effect. The German flew on towards France.

By now both angry and frustrated, MacKenzie dropped his undercarriage and pushed his throttle forward intending to hit the Messerschmitt with his undercarriage. However, the extra drag caused by the lowered wheels slowed the Hurricane so that MacKenzie began to fall behind his intended victim. Pulling the wheels back up, MacKenzie powered his fighter forward until he was alongside and slightly above the German aircraft. He then gave the control stick a swift twist so that his wing tip dropped down quickly, smashing into the tail of the Messerschmitt. The collision cost MacKenzie three feet of wing tip, but did succeed in finally forcing his enemy down into the sea.

MacKenzie had been so intent on claiming his prize that he had forgotten to keep a look out above his aircraft. No sooner had he watched the German fighter hit the sea than a cascade of machine gun bullets from two Bf109s struck his Hurricane. Without bullets he could not fight back, so MacKenzie turned for England with his throttle wide open. The Germans gave chase, firing off short bursts at the Hurricane every now and then. When MacKenzie's engine was set on fire the Messerschmitts pulled out of the attack, perhaps thinking they had secured a kill, or maybe they were short of fuel.

With his aircraft on fire and the engine losing power with every passing second, MacKenzie climbed for height. Then the engine cut out completely and the Hurricane went into a gliding dive. The undercarriage would not go down, so MacKenzie was forced to prepare for a crash-landing. He got just 300 yards past the coast before he plunged into a field, then scrambled out to safety as the fire took hold on his fighter.

MacKenzie, who already had four German aircraft to his credit before that day's events, was awarded a DFC. 'His skill and gallantry have been of the highest order' read the medal citation, with some understatement.

Typical of the men who fought gallantly without finding themselves in the media headlines was a colleague of MacKenzie's at No.501 Squadron. Sergeant Paul Farnes joined the squadron in September 1939 as a pilot and remained with the unit for more than a year. Apart from a few welcome bouts of 24 or 36 hour leave, Farnes did not take time off, but steadily and with great calmness plodded on with his duties. His name does not feature in the memoirs of other pilots with the unit, but he was there. On 9 September 1940 the squadron commander suddenly noticed that Farnes had, without any fuss or line-shooting, shot down a total of eight enemy aircraft since the war had begun a year earlier. He was recommended for, and received, a DFM. Then he went on some much-earned leave.

On 30 September two German bomber formations with fighter cover flew over Surrey on their way to London, one at 1.30 pm and the second at 4.30 pm. The subsequent fighting did not involve any fighter pilots flying from Surrey, but two German fighters from the first raid crashed there, while the second raid lost two fighters and a bomber over the county. The bomber from the second raid was claimed by the anti-aircraft guns at Gatwick, though it was finished off by fighters from outside the county. The bomber's gunner was killed and the rest of the crew were wounded. Nevertheless the pilot got the bomber down intact and the wounded men survived.

These high-speed German raiders became adept at using cloud cover to mask their approach and flight back to France. They knew that radar would alert the British to their approach over the sea, but once over land it was the Observer Corps that was responsible for tracking them. If the raiders could keep in cloud for most of their route they would be effectively invisible. They needed to pop out of the cloud every now and then to check for landmarks, but otherwise could remain hidden if the cloud cover was good enough.

In response the Observer Corps became skilled at determining the direction and rough height of an aircraft by the sound of its engines, even when it was hidden in cloud. That they could do this well was shown early in October when Pilot Officer Murch and Flight Lieutenant Duke-Woolley of No.253 Squadron were sent up from Kenley to tackle a number of bombers coming in through cloud cover.

Over the South Downs, Murch and Duke-Woolley saw a lone bomber dip out of the cloud momentarily and they turned to give chase. The bomber was soon lost in cloud again, but Duke-Woolley reported its position and asked for help. The Observer Corps spotters on the ground could see nothing, but they could hear the bomber and the fighters. By phoning back to the Operations Room their estimates of the relative positions of the three aircraft, the Observer Corps allowed the controller to guide Murch and Duke-Woolley on to the tail of the bomber. When next it dipped out of the cloud, it was right in the sights of the two Hurricane pilots, who promptly shot it down.

On 15 October No.501 Squadron was scrambled to deal with a

By 1941 many roles that had originally been filled by men were being taken over by women. This Observer Corps outpost was one of the first to have a female crew.

formation of bombers heading north over Dover towards London. There was a short battle in which the only casualty was the Hurricane of Sergeant Stanley Fenemore, an Irish volunteer, who died as his aircraft plunged into fields near Godstone.

Early in November No.253 Squadron was sent up from Kenley to deal with a daylight raid over south-east London. One Hurricane, flown by Pilot Officer Robert Watts, was shot down. Watts baled out uninjured and came floating down into a suburban street. Local residents came running with offers of tea and biscuits. Watts found himself the centre of attention and began to regale his new friends with tales of aerial battles, complete with swooping arm movements and simulated gun noises. Suddenly a little old lady pushed her way to the front of the crowd, glared up at Watts and said, 'Master Robert. Come with me. I always knew you would get yourself into trouble one of these days.' It was his former nanny.

By 1941 anti-aircraft guns were also being manned by women. At first, mixed crews were favoured with men firing the guns and women performing the support functions. However, problems with accommodation, toilet facilities and food requirements soon led to all women batteries being accepted.

On the night of 23/24 September a searchlight battery and anti-aircraft battery at Chobham had their first success of the war. At just after 1.30 am the searchlights picked up a Heinkel He111 bomber, and the adjacent guns opened fire. A shell burst close to the bomber and damaged it so badly as to make it unflyable. The pilot, Karl Niemeyer, wrestled with the controls, trying to keep the bomber steady while his crew baled out. Then he jumped through the escape hatch himself and fell clear into the cool night air over Surrey. Three of the Germans were quickly rounded up by the Home Guard, but it was not until well after dawn that the final German was found on Burhill Golf Course.

Although it is the fighter squadrons who get most of the attention, the static air defences also came under Dowding and Fighter Command HQ. For reasons that are best passed over as being complex, the searchlight batteries and barrage balloon units were part of the RAF, but the anti-aircraft guns were officially part of the army. In charge of the guns was the Irish soldier General Sir Frederick Pile. Although he was subject to operational orders from Dowding, Pile was dependent on the army for his supplies, logistical back up and resources. It was largely because Pile saw his role as supporting and assisting Dowding that the two men got on well, and because of that relationship there were no disputes between army and RAF over the deployment and use of the guns.

Although searchlights and guns could find bombers at night, the fighters could not. Spitfires and Hurricanes both relied upon the pilot being able to see the enemy aircraft for their effectiveness. But at night, the pilots simply could not see the enemy. Attempts were made, but they proved to be fruitless.

Rather more success was achieved with the two-seat fighters that had proved to be too heavy and cumbersome for daylight use when confronted by the nimble Bf109. The first of these, the turret-armed Boulton Paul Defiant, entered the fray first. While the pilot flew, the gunner was free to scan the night sky for signs of a bomber. And with four machine guns in a powered turret, the Defiant could shoot at a bomber from almost any direction. Even so, finding a victim remained a real problem.

The second failed day-fighter to go into action at night was the Blenheim 1F, and this aircraft was based in Surrey. But the Blenheim also lacked a reliable means of finding the enemy and although it had six machine guns, five of them fired forwards with only one being able to swing round in the hands of the gunner.

A searchlight probes the night sky over southern England. Like the anti-aircraft gunners, the searchlight crews came under the control of Fighter Command.

*Britain's anti-aircraft guns were under the command of General Pile,
a genial Irish soldier who managed to get on with all the
successive commanders of Fighter Command.*

On 7 September 1940 No.600 Squadron equipped with Blenheim 1F night-fighters took up residence at Redhill airfield. Dowding gave the squadron a dreadful report when he wrote, 'The importance of getting aircraft into the air at the earliest possible moment has been difficult to instill into No.600 Squadron, who have been inclined to apply peacetime standards to a serious war situation. I hope to have no more cause for criticism in this respect.' To be fair to the men of No.600 the skills of night-fighting were proving difficult for everyone to master.

On 12 October, No.600 Squadron left Redhill to be replaced by No.219 Squadron. The new arrivals had Blenheim 1F night-fighters, but they also had the newer, faster and more powerful Bristol Beaufighter 1F. On the night of 25 October, No.219 Squadron got its first confirmed success when Sergeant Hodgkinson attacked a German bomber that was threatening Kenley. His gunfire had an immediate effect, as the bomber

A flight of Boulton Paul Defiant fighters. The concept of a turret-armed fighter proved useless against nimble Bf109 fighters, but the design was more of a success in the night-fighter role.

Key ingredients in the success of the Beaufighter were the massively powerful Bristol Hercules engines which developed around 1600 horsepower.

turned away and fled south. The bomber was tracked by the Observer Corps and was seen to crash in flames just off the coast.

No.219 Squadron did not get everything its own way. On the night of 14 October a Beaufighter from the squadron got lost over the blacked out county after suffering electrical failure that knocked out the radio and other equipment. Unable to see where to land the two-man crew baled out. The aircraft crashed near Send. Two nights later a second No.219 night-fighter, this time a Blenheim 1F crashed on landing when the pilot, Sergeant H. Grubb, misjudged his position and crashed into the perimeter fence and hedge. He walked away from the prang, but the aircraft was written off.

About this time the Operations Room for RAF Kenley was moved from its rather cramped, converted butcher's shop to The Grange, a large 17th-century house in Coulsdon. With the additional space available, the

Kenley Sector was chosen by Dowding for the trial run of an experimental method of tracking bombers over land at night. The man chosen to conduct the trials was Major Russell, the army officer responsible for anti-aircraft guns in the Kenley Sector.

For some months a short-range radar, code-named 'George', had been in operation to help searchlights locate bombers in the night sky. This short-range radar could give the bearing and height of an aircraft, allowing the master searchlight, to which it was attached, to pick out the bomber. The other searchlights in the battery would then lock on to the aircraft so that it was caught by a cone of several beams that would be more difficult for the pilot to shake off than a single beam. The guns could then aim at the aircraft in the hope of bringing it down.

Dowding's plan was to extend the range of the George radar sets so that they overlapped to create a mesh of interlocking fields of radar cover that embraced the whole area of sky over the Kenley Sector. In theory it would

The need to inflict maximum damage during the brief shooting opportunities of night-fighting led to the Beaufighter having a massive armament of four cannon and six machine guns.

be possible for the radar operators to track a bomber as it came in over the sea, then alert the nearest George crew to its arrival. That George crew would track the bomber as it passed over its area, passing the task on to the next crew as the aircraft flew out of range. Each crew would telephone the bomber's position and movements back to the Operations Room where its track would be marked on the map. Meanwhile, the location of any night-fighter could be tracked by means of its pip-squeak equipment. The Controller could then direct the night-fighter to bring it close enough for the pilot to see the target – at least on reasonably bright nights if there was plenty of moonlight or starlight available.

The George system was fairly successful, but what was really needed was a night-fighter equipped with its own airborne radar. Dowding had foreseen the need for such a combination. He had sponsored and encouraged the development of airborne radar and an aircraft – the Bristol Beaufighter – to carry it. The new weapon entered service with two squadrons in September 1940 and on 20 November got its first success when a Junkers Ju88 bomber was shot down in pitch darkness by a Beaufighter equipped with airborne radar.

Four days later Dowding, the man who had created Fighter Command and led it to victory, was removed from the organisation. The suddenness of his removal and the way he was treated have been the subject of huge controversy. It is true that he had been due for retirement more than a year earlier and that he had held the post longer than was normal in the RAF at this time. However, the swift way in which he was pushed aside and the fact that he was not given either promotion or some other reward was unusual. When Park was shifted from command of 11 Group at the same time there was a feeling that there had been a deliberate purge at the top of Fighter Command.

It has since transpired that Leigh-Mallory, the commander of 12 Group, had put a lot of effort into seeking to discredit Dowding and Park at the Air Ministry and that he had cultivated friendships with politicians of the day. Leigh-Mallory was to die before the war ended, so he was not around to give his side of events when the history of Fighter Command came to be written, so the blame that was heaped on him by supporters of Park and Dowding might be a bit unfair. Nevertheless he replaced Park at 11 Group and at once began making his idea of the Big Wing a reality by reorganising the Group around this tactical innovation.

There could, at least, be no complaints about the quality of Dowding's

*The statue of Air Chief Marshal Lord Dowding that stands outside
St Clement Danes Church in London.*

Air Chief Marshal William Sholto Douglas took over Fighter Command in the autumn of 1940. He reorganised the force around three squadron wings and put it on to the offensive, sending out numerous sweeps over France. In 1944 he took over Coastal Command and launched a successful anti-U-boat campaign. He retired from the RAF in 1946 to take over as Chairman of British European Airways (BEA), one of the more successful post-war civil airlines. He died in 1969.

Bristol Beaufighter 1f

Type: Twin seat night-fighter
Engine: 2 x 1400 Bristol Hercules III
Wingspan: 57 ft 10 in
Length: 41 ft 4 in
Height: 15 ft 10 in
Weight: Empty 14,069 lb
Loaded 21,100 lb
Armament: 4 x 20 mm cannon in nose plus 6 x .303 machine guns in wings
Max speed: 323 mph
Ceiling: 28,900 ft
Range: 1170 miles
Production: 5,584

The superb Beaufighter grew out of the equally impressive Beaufort, a long-range bomber developed for Coastal Command that could carry a torpedo as an alternative to conventional bombs. It entered production late in 1939 with the first aircraft reaching Fighter Command in October 1940. The concept was to have a fighter large enough to carry an air-to-air radar set and a second crew member to operate it. The designers assumed that there would be time for only a short burst of fire at a target, hence the heavy armament. The Beaufighter was later modified to be an anti-shipping strike aircraft able to carry either rockets or a torpedo in addition to its cannon. The unusually quiet engines of this aircraft caused it to be nicknamed 'whispering death' by the Japanese.

The Beaufighter 1f entered RAF service with the Fighter Interception Unit at RAF Tangmere on 12 August 1940. The first operation by the type was conducted on the night of 4/5 September; later that month the new night-fighter made its operational service with Nos.25, 29, 219 and 604 Squadrons. It was the last of these units that scored the type's first 'kill' using AI Mk IV radar when a Ju88 was downed on 19 November 1940. Subsequent development in the night-fighter role led to the Beaufighter IIf and VIf, both of which eventually gave way to night-fighter versions of the de Havilland Mosquito.

successor. Air Chief Marshal William Sholto Douglas had won both the DFC and the Military Cross as a pilot during the First World War. He had been Deputy Chief of the Air Staff throughout the Battle of Britain and was a relatively youthful 47 years old.

Whatever the circumstances under which Sholto Douglas came to command Fighter Command, it was clear that the battles to be fought in the future would be very different to those of 1940. With an invasion of Britain no longer likely, Fighter Command and the RAF in general was going to be on the offensive. Sholto Douglas was the man for the job.

Chapter 8

Eagles Over France

Over the winter of 1940–41, the Luftwaffe bombers continued their nocturnal pounding of London and other cities. Daylight raiders came over in small groups and at high speed to make precision raids on individual targets. Fighter Command, and increasing numbers of night-fighters in particular, were kept busy dealing with these intruders.

The new head of Fighter Command, Sholto Douglas, was determined to go on the offensive. That meant going over to France. As yet the British had no realistic hope of invading the Continent and although successes were being scored in the Mediterranean area against Italy, it was not entirely clear how Germany was to be defeated. Nevertheless, something had to be done to show that Britain was still in the war and fighting aggressively.

Sholto Douglas began to adopt tactics remarkably similar to those employed by the Luftwaffe in the autumn of 1940. While RAF Bomber Command was slowly building up its force to the point where it could raid targets in Germany at night with some degree of success, more immediate advantages could be expected by attacking German military bases and transport hubs in the occupied countries. Sholto Douglas began a series of offensive operations that would consume much of Fighter Command's efforts during 1941, 1942 and much of 1943.

As time passed these operations came to be known by designated

*A squadron of Hurricanes sets out on a sweep over northern France,
watched by a ploughman in a field below.*

codenames, though in the early days this terminology was not always strictly adhered to.

A Rhubarb was a raid carried out by two or three fighters that would fly over an area of the Continent looking for targets of opportunity. Most Rhubarbs were organised at squadron level. A Rodeo was similar to a Rhubarb, but carried out by one or more squadrons of fighters acting together. Rodeos needed to be approved at Group level. A Ramrod involved fighters flying as escort to a bombing raid on a specific target. A Circus was similar to a Ramrod but with a vast fighter escort that hoped to draw up and ambush Luftwaffe fighters. A Jim Crow was a routine patrol, usually over the sea, to look for enemy activity and help to preserve RAF control of the air space.

Sholto Douglas also introduced changes to the way Fighter Command was organised. Instead of the squadrons being answerable directly to Group, he introduced an intermediate formation: the Wing. This was based on Leigh-Mallory's idea of a Big Wing combat formation, but adapted to the needs of the RAF administrative set up. Each Wing consisted of three squadrons of fighters, at least one of which was a Spitfire squadron, under a Wing Commander. Where possible the Wing was based on a single airfield; but if not, on bases that were close together. It was envisaged that these Wings would cooperate in training and combat becoming proficient at flying together when attacking the enemy.

These changes had an effect on the ground in Surrey. Kenley became the home base for the Kenley Wing, but it was not large enough for three squadrons so one was based at Croydon. Croydon soon proved to be unsuitable and was gradually wound down as a Fighter Command base, being handed over to squadrons training for ground attack and army cooperation. Instead Redhill was upgraded with the addition of a concrete perimeter track and blister hangars, though the runway remained grass for the time being. Gatwick was abandoned by Fighter Command in January 1941 and it, like Croydon, was passed to army support squadrons.

It was not until the summer that the Kenley Wing settled down to consist of three Spitfire squadrons: No.452, No.485 and No.602. In charge was Wing Commander John Peel while his deputy, the New Zealander Al Deere, also commanded No.602 Squadron.

Deere had first entered combat in May 1940 when he flew escort to transport aircraft heading for France as the panzers stormed forward and the skies swarmed with Luftwaffe aircraft. On 23 May he shot down two

The RAF Croydon Monument on the site of the former airfield.

Messerschmitt Bf109 fighters within ten minutes, and a third later that same day. Three Bf110 fighters went down to his guns in the next two days, but he was then shot down and crash-landed his Spitfire on a beach. He then stole a bike and pedalled to Dunkirk to be evacuated. Shot down later in the Battle of Britain, Deere baled out but his parachute failed to open properly. Convinced that he was about to die, Deere closed his eyes as the ground loomed up towards him. He landed in a farm cesspool and emerged unscathed, though stinking horribly. Arriving back at Kenley, Deere managed to shoot down a Bf109 on his first day – a feat which immediately endeared him to his men.

Wing Commander John Peel commanded the Kenley Wing for most of 1941. He was awarded the DSO for his inspired leadership, but was better known in the RAF for having fired the first shot during the Battle of Britain.

In April 1942 Deere was to leave Kenley to go to the USA to train fighter pilots in modern air combat tactics. He returned to combat flying in 1943, but did not serve in Surrey as he took over the Wing based at Biggin Hill. After the war he served as station commander at Duxford and, after various promotions and postings, retired in 1967. He ended his career with the DFC and bar, DSO, OBE, the American DFC and the Croix de Guerre from France. He died in 1995.

Among the men serving at Kenley under Deere was the Irish ace Brendan Finucane, known inevitably as Paddy, who had already shot down five German aircraft and been awarded a DFC by the time he came to Kenley. When Deere recommended Finucane for a bar to his DFC in September 1941 he wrote 'This officer has been largely responsible for the fine fighting spirit of the unit'.

Finucane had the odd ability to go for weeks without so

much as firing his guns and then spend a day or two in the grip of a fighting frenzy of epic proportions. In the space of two days in September 1941 he came back from leave, went up to shoot down three Messerschmitts in a single dogfight, came back to Kenley for a night's sleep then went out on a dawn patrol to shoot down two more.

In October he was leading his section when they were bounced by a group of Bf109 fighters. One of the Germans got on to the tail of a Spitfire, so Finucane went to attack the German from behind, only to find a second Bf109 on his own tail. Seconds later another No.452 Squadron Spitfire got behind that German and all five aircraft were chasing each other around the sky. The combat ended with both German fighters going down. Finucane and his colleagues then turned round to find the rest of the German force fleeing at high speed.

Finucane's epic fighting career at Kenley came to an end when he was leaving the Greyhound pub in nearby Croydon after a night out to celebrate his 15th kill. In the blackout, and perhaps rather the worse for drink, Finucane tripped over a low wall and fell into a hole, breaking his ankle as he landed. Finucane later returned to combat, though not in Surrey. His score had reached 32 when he was shot down and killed on 15 July 1942. As he went down he radioed to his squadron comrades the final message 'I think this is it chaps'.

In February 1942 the Kenley Wing sparked a major operation with a routine patrol over the Channel flown by Victor Beamish and Finlay Boyd. The two pilots were just off Cap Gris Nez at 11.15 am when they spotted a number of craft through the clouds. Beamish and Boyd went down to attack, strafing what turned out to be E-boats and causing one to sink. When German destroyers with heavy anti-aircraft guns appeared the two Spitfire pilots climbed back up into the cloud. Thinking the presence of destroyers rather unusual, but under strict radio-silence orders, the pilots raced back to Kenley to report. That prompted the RAF to send off a reconnaissance aircraft which explored the area to discover the amazing fact that two of Germany's most powerful warships were steaming through the Channel in broad daylight.

The ships in question were the *Scharnhorst* and *Gneisenau*, a pair of battle cruisers or pocket battleships of 31,000 tons armed with nine 11 inch guns each. These warships had been built to be high-speed commerce raiders in the Atlantic. They had the firepower to destroy

Brendan 'Paddy' Finucane was one of the most successful fighter pilots in the RAF. He was flying out of Kenley when he was awarded a bar to his DFC. He had shot down a total of 32 enemy aircraft by the time he was killed in the summer of 1942.

anything they could not outrun and the speed to catch anything they did not outgun. These formidable ships had sunk 22 vessels from a single convoy in February 1941. They had since then been kept in Brest, a constant threat to the Atlantic convoy routes. Although they had never again attacked a convoy they only had to put to sea to have the Royal Navy cancel convoys and send those at sea back to port. The RAF had frequently tried to bomb them, but without success. The news that they were at sea galvanised the navy and the RAF.

The first aircraft to get into the air to attack the warships were six Fairey Swordfish torpedo aircraft of the Fleet Air Arm. The Kenley Wing was ordered to send up every fighter that could fly as an escort to the slow biplanes. Sadly the weather over Dover was by this point so atrocious that the Spitfires failed to find either the Swordfish or the German battle

By 1942 the Luftwaffe was busy deep inside Russia and raids on Britain fell in number. However the role of the Observer Corps remained important as high-speed, low-level daylight raids remained capable of inflicting damage on targets south of the Thames.

cruisers. The Swordfish found their targets and attacked, but all six were shot down.

Having landed to refuel, the Kenley Wing was sent out again. This time they found the destroyers that Boyd and Beamish had seen earlier. The Spitfires went down to strafe, but did not inflict any serious damage, though they did succeed in shooting down three Bf109 fighters that were circling overhead as a protective cover. Other bombing attacks were made, but without much success in the the dreadful weather, and Royal Navy destroyers tried to attack but sustained damage and were driven off. *Scharnhorst* and *Gneisenau* got to Germany having suffered only minor damage.

By this time a new threat was emerging over the skies of France – the Focke Wulf FW190. This superb fighter was faster and more nimble than the Spitfire MkV being flown by the Kenley Wing, while its armament of four 20mm cannon and two machine guns was terrifyingly powerful.

On 28 March Kenley suffered its first casualty at the guns of the FW190, and it was a profound loss. Group Captain Victor Beamish DFC, was one of the most popular officers on the base and had just been promoted to have overall command of the Kenley Sector. Although his rank and age, he was 39, meant that he did not need to fly into combat, he chose to do so in order to boost morale among his men and to keep up his understanding of combat conditions. He was on a Rodeo with No.485 Squadron when the force was bounced by FW190 fighters. Beamish's Spitfire went down into the Channel. Although the entire Wing took off to try to find him in his dinghy, he was never sighted.

The Wing was plunged into gloom by the loss. 'Here, indeed, was a man,' recorded the official Station Record Book.

A few weeks later, on 29 April, King George VI paid an unannounced and unexpected call on Kenley to watch at first hand a Circus operation take place. He arrived soon after the Wing had taken off, and watched the operation unfold on the map at the Operations Room in The Grange while listening to the radio chatter between the pilots. When the Wing returned, fortunately without loss, the King insisted on being introduced to every single pilot, even waiting while those who had landed at Redhill were brought over by bus. Morale was restored, but Beamish was not forgotten.

The arrival of the FW190 in 1942 came as a nasty shock to the RAF. The new fighter was superior to anything the RAF could field at the time.

Group Captain Victor Beamish was one of the most popular officers to serve at RAF Kenley, taking over command of the Sector in 1942. After he was shot down and killed his comrades renamed the main road through the base in his honour. Although the airbase has gone, the road name remains (opposite page).

His place was taken by Group Captain David Atcherly DFC, who had three enemy aircraft to his credit and was a highly experienced night-fighter. He was not familiar with the Spitfire so he decided to take one up to practice on and was promptly shot down into the Channel by an FW190. He escaped with only scratches and was back in his office later that same day.

In July 1942 several squadrons of the United States Army Air Force (USAAF) came to Kenley for a few days at a time. They were equipped with Spitfire MkV fighters and came to Kenley so that the experienced pilots there could teach them modern combat tactics and explain to them how the Germans fought. Most of the American squadrons were commanded by an RAF Squadron Leader during their training and were passed fit for combat only when that officer was convinced that they were ready.

Despite this, emergencies could arise and it was because of one of these that the USAAF 308th Fighter Squadron went into battle commanded by Squadron Leader Peter Wickham on 19 August 1942. On that day a massive amphibious assault took place on the French port of Dieppe.

The purpose of the Dieppe raid was threefold. First, it was designed to test out different tactics and ideas about launching a seaborne landing against a defended coast. Second, it aimed to destroy German naval and military facilities in the port town and third, it was intended that the attack would convince the Germans that an invasion of France from Britain would be taking place soon. It was hoped that the Germans would therefore move troops to France and then relieve pressure on the Russians.

At least it would allow the British government to tell Stalin that they were doing something practical by way of help.

The ground raid was carried out mainly by Canadians, about 5,000 of whom landed at Dieppe backed up by tanks and by the guns of the Royal Navy. The fighter squadrons from Kenley, including 308th FS, were to join the massed formations of Fighter Command over Dieppe with the aim of seizing and retaining control of the sky over the town and adjacent areas for the duration of the raid.

In the event the air side of the raid went well. The fighters drove off every effort by German aircraft to intervene. But on the ground the raid went disastrously wrong as landing tactics failed and German defences were stronger than expected. The Canadians lost 3,500 of their 5,000 men.

One of those to have taken part in both the Channel Dash and Dieppe battles was the quiet New Zealand pilot John Checketts, then a Pilot Officer. When he came to Kenley, Checketts had shot down no enemy aircraft, nor so much as damaged one. He had, however, been shot down

A staged propaganda photo shows the elements of the air-sea rescue service operated by the RAF during the Battle of Britain. If the pilot baled out and took to his dinghy, his comrades would radio a rough position. A Lysander, as here, or similar scout aircraft would take off to locate the dinghy before it had time to drift, and then circle until a rescue craft could approach.

himself – though he baled out safely. While at Kenley he continued to have no luck at all, rarely firing his guns and never hitting anything. And he came home once in a Spitfire so badly shot up that it had to be scrapped.

Towards the end of 1942 Checketts came to the end of his tour of duty and was sent off on six months' non-combat duty. He was determined to do better when he came back to operational duties. He spent his time flying at every possible opportunity and spending day after day practising air gunnery. As a result he came back to Kenley not only rested, but much improved as a fighter pilot.

It was now the spring of 1943 and on one of his first patrols over France he ran into an FW190. With newly acquired skills, Checketts got on the tail of the German and let rip with the uprated twin 20 mm cannon and four machine guns of the Spitfire MkIX that he was flying. The tail of the FW190 was blasted off and the fighter ploughed into the ground and exploded. 'It upset me quite considerably,' Checketts said later. 'He was somebody's boy with a mother and father. But I also thought it could easily have been me. After that I didn't let it worry me because it was him or me.'

Indeed, it did not. Checketts rose steadily through the ranks just as his tally of downed Germans climbed. On 9 August 1943 he led his section of four Spitfires into a dogfight with eight Bf109 fighters. He shot down four of the Germans while his comrades finished off the rest. That action resulted in the award of a DFC and he was later to win the DSO. He soon rose to be Commanding Officer of No.285 Squadron.

On 6 September 1943 Checketts was leading his squadron in a sweep over France when they ran into a force of 20 FW190 fighters. The Spitfires were outnumbered, but fought back gallantly. Checketts himself shot down one German, but then his engine exploded and flames engulfed the Spitfire. He baled out and had the good fortune to land on a farm owned by a Frenchman in touch with the Resistance. He was given rough first aid to the burns on his face and hands before being bundled off to stay with another French family some distance from where his aircraft had crashed.

A map showing the main features of the disastrous Dieppe raid.
Fighter Command successfully beat off Luftwaffe attacks and was one of
the few sections to come out of the event well.

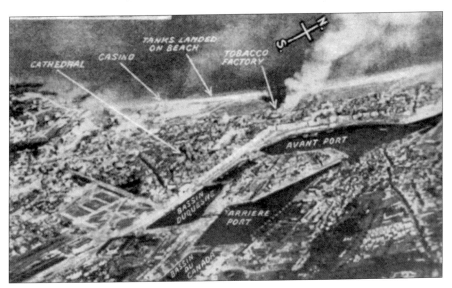

Wing Commander 'Johnnie' Johnson was one of the highest scoring fighter aces in the RAF. Exactly how many aircraft he shot down is not known as by this date he routinely allowed his victims to be credited to other men in his squadron in order to boost their confidence and morale.

One night three weeks later a French man entered Checketts' room and beckoned him to follow. The pair walked for miles until they reached a small fishing harbour. Checketts was wordlessly led aboard a small fishing boat and gently shoved down below. There he was guided past a large storage tub for the lobsters the boat caught and into a hidden compartment that stank badly of fish and was ankle deep in water. A couple of days later two more RAF men joined him. Then some more. After 12 days, no fewer than ten RAF men were crammed into the hidden compartment that was only ten feet by three. Eventually the lobster boat put to sea. It spent the first two days catching lobsters, then dodged patrolling German E-boats to dart across the Channel to put into Mousehole in Cornwall. The RAF men were hurriedly ejected and the lobster boat headed back towards France before it was missed.

When he recovered from his burns, Checketts was promoted to Wing Commander and took over a three-squadron Spitfire wing that was

A Beaufighter equipped with rockets for ground attack duties.
The black and white stripes were painted on for D-Day so that nervous
ground troops would know friend from foe.

providing cover for the D-Day invasion force. He ended the war with a confirmed 14 kills, 15 probables, 2 V1 flying bombs and two E-boats to his credit. He was awarded the Polish Star of Valour for his work with Polish squadrons later in the war. When peace came he returned to New Zealand to join the RNZAF. He retired in 1955 to take up farming and died in 2006 aged 94. The RNZAF managed to find a Second World War vintage fighter to perform a fly past at his funeral.

One of the lessons that the RAF learned from the Dieppe raid was that fuel endurance was of paramount importance. Combat flying consumed fuel a lot more quickly than did patrolling; also the time taken to fly to and from the French coast had to be taken into account. Frequent changes of squadron patrolling over enemy air space was going to be needed if air cover was to be guaranteed.

As planning for the D-Day landings of 1944 began it was decided that those fighter squadrons that would be needed to patrol over the landing

Focke Wulf FW190

Type: Fighter
Engine: 1 x 1700 hp BMW 801D
Wingspan: 34 ft 5 in
Length: 29 ft
Height: 13 ft
Weight: Empty 6,393 lb
Loaded 8,770 lb
Armament: 2 x 7.9 machine guns in nose plus 4 x 20 mm
cannon in wings
Max speed: 382 mph
Ceiling: 35,000 ft
Range: 500 miles
Production: 20,051

Without doubt Germany's finest fighter of the war, the Focke Wulf FW190 first flew in June 1939 but problems with the engine meant it did not enter combat in any numbers until the end of 1941. It proved to be fast and nimble, easily outclassing all Allied fighters – even the Spitfire MkV which had only just entered service. The British rushed the Spitfire IX into production, but this took time and only matched the FW190 in combat conditions. By the end of 1942 half of all German fighters being produced were FW190s, designed in a number of variants to carry bombs or torpedoes as well as the standard fighter armament. In 1944 a variant, the FW190D, was produced with a Junkers Jumo 213 engine. This aircraft proved to be a magnificent high-altitude fighter and took a heavy toll on American daylight bombers operating above 30,000 ft. The FW190G was a ground attack variant able to carry up to 4,000 lb of bombs to a range of 220 miles from base.

The first FW190As were delivered to Jagdgeschwader 26 in August 1941 and within weeks the Würger ('Butcher Bird'), as the new fighter was nicknamed, came up against RAF Fighter Command Spitfires for the first time. The FW190A was built in nine production models (A-1 to A-9) with numerous sub-variants configured for various roles.

beaches and enforce Allied air superiority over the inland areas would need to be based much closer to the landing beaches. A rapid programme of airfield construction was put in hand. Temporary fighter bases, known as Advance Landing Grounds (ALG) were built along the south coast of England. The squadrons of fighters that had been based in Surrey for so long moved on.

A new chapter in the history of Fighter Command in Surrey was about to begin.

Chapter 9

Bomber Offensive

A **s the old squadrons flew out,** the new ones came in. Kenley and Redhill were now the only fighter bases operating in Surrey. In place of the departing squadrons came the Canadian Wing which at various times was composed of various Canadian squadrons, including Nos. 401, 402, 403, 412, 416 and 421. The commander of these largely new and untried squadrons was the veteran RAF ace James 'Johnnie' Johnson.

Johnson had missed the Battle of Britain due to a broken collarbone, but had quickly made up for lost time when he entered service in 1941. He served at first under Douglas Bader in Sussex, becoming an expert at cross-Channel fighter sweeps. He fought over Dieppe and his score of downed German aircraft was approaching 20 when he was posted to command the Canadians.

At this date the Canadians had a reputation for being tough and enthusiastic fighters when serving in British RAF squadrons, but for being relatively poor at organisation and discipline when formed into units of their own. Johnson was nervous about his new command. His feelings were not improved when, soon after he arrived, he received a visit from the Canadian Syd Ford, commander of No.403 Squadron. Ford walked into Johnson's office and slapped a pair of blue 'Canada' shoulder flashes on to his desk. 'The boys would like you to wear these,'

Wing Commander 'Johnnie' Johnson came to RAF Kenley in 1943 to take command of the newly formed Canadian Wing. He proved to be so popular with the 'Canucks' that the Canadian government later insisted that he be put in charge of the Canadian squadrons serving in Britain.

he announced. 'After all, we are a Canadian wing and we've got to convert you. Better start now.' Johnson gamely had the flashes sewn on to his uniform.

In the event, Johnson need not have worried. The Canadians under his command proved to be as capable at administration and discipline as they were at fighting. Sergeant H. Morrow of No.403 Squadron was returning from a sweep over France when the engine of his Spitfire suddenly packed up due to some unsuspected damage. Looking around for somewhere to land he spotted a field near Winchelsea in Sussex and dived down. Unfortunately the field proved to be shorter than he thought. After careering over the turf the Spitfire plunged through a fence, lost its undercarriage in a ditch, skidded over a road, burst through a hedge and finally came to a halt in a wood. Looking around, Morrow realised that both wings of his Spitfire had been torn off, as had the tail. But the radio was still working. He called up his squadron leader and using perfectly correct procedural language announced that he was down and safe but that his aircraft was damaged. He then hopped out of the wreck and went to the New Inn in the village for a drink.

By the time the Canadian Wing arrived late in 1943 the air war had changed again. The night skies over Surrey were now filled with RAF bombers setting off to pound the Reich, or with those same aircraft coming back. Some of those bombers were badly damaged and put down on Surrey airfields in desperation. Some of those that came down on Kenley were unable to take off again from the short runway and had to be broken up and taken away by lorry. On 19 April 1944 the Canadian Wing left Kenley. The station's days as a fighter base were over.

Meanwhile a new temporary fighter base had opened in the south of the county at Horne. The Wing Commander in charge was an old Surrey hand, the New Zealander John Checketts, now boasting a DSO and DFC on his tunic. The primary task of the three Spitfire squadrons was to fly long, gruelling and frequently repeated patrols along the Sussex coast to stop German reconnaissance aircraft from spying on the Allies' preparations for D-Day. Action was infrequent, but exhaustion and boredom were permanent problems. The dull routine was made worse by the fact that RAF Horne had no proper buildings, being merely a grass airstrip surrounded by tents. Men had to go to a nearby school to get a hot bath.

On D-Day itself the Horne Wing patrolled at low level over the landing beaches and adjacent areas of sea. They saw no action. A week later the Spitfires moved out and Horne was demobilised.

For Fighter Command in Surrey, the war was over. But it was not forgotten. Croydon reverted to civilian use in 1946 after a period as a military transportation hub. A magnificent memorial to the pilots of Fighter Command who served there was erected just south of the main airport entrance on what is now Purley Way. The airport closed in 1959, but the memorial remains, as do the control tower and the famous Aerodrome Hotel, a triumph of 1920s' architecture. At Kenley there is

An American B17 Flying Fortress bombs a target in northern France.
During 1943 the fighters based in Surrey increasingly flew escort to these raids.

Most of the wartime features of RAF Kenley have long since been demolished, but this blast shelter remains near the eastern edge of the airfield.

The runway of RAF Kenley as it is today. During the Battle of Britain this was a grass airfield, the concrete runway was added later in the war and today serves the local ATC and a gliding club.

also a memorial to the men and women of Fighter Command, and rather more of the airfield can still be seen. The old runways and perimeter track still exist, and flying still takes place here – albeit mostly gliders.

The contribution made by Fighter Command squadrons based in Surrey was immense. During the hectic, costly combats fought during the Battle of Britain the pilots went up time after time, often several times a day. Those on the ground were no less busy as they kept the aircraft and pilots in fighting trim. Their role was no less dangerous when the German bombers swept in to deal out death and destruction.

*The crowded skies over a landing site for glider troops on D-Day, 6 June 1944.
Surrey-based fighters flew numerous missions to cover the invasion force.
Within a few weeks of D-Day the need for fighters based in Surrey had gone.*

The RAF Kenley Monument. It is dedicated to all those who served at Kenley during the war and is engraved with the numbers of all the squadrons and other units that were based here.

If any body of men and women can claim to have saved Britain from Nazi invasion during the Second World War, it is those who served in RAF Fighter Command, Surrey.

Index

Squadrons